Table of Contents

Title Page

Copyright

Front Matter

Table of Contents

Introduction: Contemplating the Cosmos through Faith

The Universe as Creation

Understanding Cosmology and Catholic Teaching

The Universe: Signs of God's Grandeur

God, the First Cause and Final End

Genesis, Cosmology, and the Catholic Perspective

Interpreting Genesis in the Age of Space Exploration

The Ethical Imperatives of Exploring the Heavens

The Morality of Reaching Beyond Earth

Stewardship of the Universe: A Catholic Duty

The Church's Role in the Age of Cosmic Exploration

Catholicism and the Dialogue with Science

Pioneers of Faith in the Space Era

Humanity's Place Among the Stars

The Call to Expand Horizons

Respecting Creation While Embracing the Cosmos

Space Exploration and the Common Good

Pursuing Knowledge for Humanity's Benefit

The Dangers of Exploitation in Space

The Saints and the Stars: Spiritual Guidance on Our Cosmic Journey

Lessons from Saints for Modern Cosmologists

Finding God in the Vastness of Space

Providence and the Physical Universe

Understanding Divine Providence in Creation

The Limits of Human Control in the Cosmos

Ethical Boundaries in Colonizing Other Worlds

Respecting Alien Worlds and Their Potential Inhabitants

The Concept of "Space as a Common Home"

Catholicism and the Multiplanetary Human Species

Theological Considerations of Living Beyond Earth

Salvation History Extended to Other Planets

Ecological Ethics in Space Exploration

Catholic Social Teachings and Sustainability in Space

Maintaining Ecological Balance Across the Cosmos

The Church and the Future of Space Travel

Contributions of Catholic Thought to Interstellar Ethics

Guiding Principles for Future Missions

Looking Heavenward with Hope and Responsibility

Catholic Documents on Science and the Universe

Glossary of Terms in Cosmology and Catholic Theology

The Heavens Proclaim the Altar of the Stars: Catholicism and the
Ethical Boundaries of Space

Contents

Introduction: Contemplating the Cosmos through Faith

The Universe as Creation

Understanding Cosmology and Catholic Teaching

Chapter 2: God, the First Cause and Final End

Genesis, Cosmology, and the Catholic Perspective

The Ethical Imperatives of Exploring the Heavens

The Morality of Reaching Beyond Earth

The Church's Role in the Age of Cosmic Exploration

Catholicism and the Dialogue with Science

Humanity's Place Among the Stars

The Call to Expand Horizons

Chapter 6: Space Exploration and the Common Good

Pursuing Knowledge for Humanity's Benefit

The Saints and the Stars: Spiritual Guidance on Our Cosmic Journey

Lessons from Saints for Modern Cosmologists

Providence and the Physical Universe

Understanding Divine Providence in Creation

Ethical Boundaries in Colonizing Other Worlds

Respecting Alien Worlds and Their Potential Inhabitants

Catholicism and the Multiplanetary Human Species

Theological Considerations of Living Beyond Earth

Chapter 11: Ecological Ethics in Space Exploration

Catholic Social Teachings and Sustainability in Space

The Church and the Future of Space Travel

Contributions of Catholic Thought to Interstellar Ethics

Looking Heavenward with Hope and Responsibility

Appendix A: Catholic Documents on Science and the Universe

Glossary of Terms in Cosmology and Catholic Theology

References

Introduction: Contemplating the Cosmos through Faith

The cosmos, in its vast expanse and incomprehensible grandeur, holds a mirror up to the human soul, reflecting not only what we are but what we aspire to be. It stretches out, seemingly infinite, heavy with mysteries that have perplexed humanity since the dawn of consciousness. As we stand on the precipice of becoming a multiplanetary species, our contemplation of the cosmos through faith is not only timely but essential. This book seeks to bridge the seemingly vast chasm between the empirical quests of cosmology and the spiritual journey of faith, specifically within the rich traditions of Roman Catholic teaching.

At the heart of this exploration is the understanding that space exploration and the Catholic faith are not mutually exclusive endeavors but are, in fact, complementary pathways to understanding our place in the universe. The Catholic tradition, with its deep reverence for the act of creation and the Creator, provides a rich framework for contemplating the cosmos. The book aims to explicate that God, as the almighty creator and the final end of all creation, has fashioned the universe in a manner that beckons humanity to explore, understand, and ultimately find Him within the vast reaches of space.

Space exploration serves as a modern chapter in humanity's perennial quest to understand the cosmos. It aligns with the Catholic teaching that sees the pursuit of scientific knowledge as a form of participation in the divine act of creation. This perspective invites us to reflect on the role of Divine Providence in the unfolding universe. It reminds us that every discovery and every effort to stretch beyond our earthly confines is part of a larger, divinely orchestrated narrative.

Through the Gospel and perennial Catholic teaching, this book endeavors to present space exploration as a profoundly spiritual journey. It posits that the ethical imperatives of exploring the heavens, far from being an adjunct to the scientific endeavor, are central to our calling as stewards of creation. The Catholic duty towards creation is not limited to Earth but extends to the entire cosmos, challenging us to approach the heavens with both awe and a sense of responsibility.

The dialogue between Catholicism and the cosmos is not new; it is deeply rooted in the Church's history and tradition. This book reinvigorates that dialogue, interpreting the age-old wisdom of the Church in the light of contemporary cosmological discoveries. It asserts the Church's role in the age of cosmic exploration, not as a bystander but as a proactive participant, guiding humanity's steps into the unknown with moral clarity and spiritual insight.

Humanity's place among the stars, as seen through the lens of Catholic teaching, offers a unique vantage point. It reminds us that while we aspire to reach other worlds, our ultimate end is transcendent. The book delineates how the pursuit of knowledge, the drive to explore, and the longing to discover are not merely human traits but divine calls to action. These efforts serve the common good, drawing humanity closer together and closer to God in the process.

The inherent dangers of space exploration, including the potential for exploitation and the ethical dilemmas posed by colonizing other worlds, are also considered. The book calls for an ethical approach grounded in Catholic social teachings, emphasizing respect for creation and the concept of space as a common home.

The theological implications of living beyond Earth pose profound questions for Catholic theology. This book tackles those questions, expanding the horizons of salvation history to include our eventual life among the stars. It discusses how the Church can extend its pastoral mission to other planets, ensuring that as humanity spreads through the cosmos, it carries with it the light of the Gospel.

In contemplating the cosmos through faith, we are reminded of the delicate balance between human effort and divine providence. This book elucidates the Catholic understanding of providence in the act of creation, emphasizing that while humans are co-creators with God, we must always acknowledge the limits of our control and the supremacy of divine will.

The final frontier of space offers not only new worlds to explore but also new ethical challenges. This book discusses the Church's role in establishing ethical boundaries for colonizing other worlds, ensuring that respect for the integrity of creation is maintained. It highlights the Church's potential contributions to interstellar ethics, suggesting guiding principles for future missions.

In conclusion, as we look heavenward, our vision of the cosmos is expanded not just by the telescopes and spacecraft but by faith. This book argues that Catholic thought, with its deep understanding of creation, providence, and the moral order, has much to contribute to humanity's cosmic journey. It is a journey that is not just about reaching new planets but about understanding our place in the cosmos and drawing closer to the Creator.

In this age of unparalleled discoveries and the dawn of interplanetary travel, let us contemplate the cosmos through the lens of faith. May our exploration of the heavens, guided by the wisdom of the Catholic Church, lead us to a deeper understanding of creation and our Creator, grounding our scientific ambitions in the rich soil of spiritual tradition.

Through this synthesis of faith and reason, may we approach the cosmos not as conquerors but as humble pilgrims, seeking not only new horizons but deeper truths about ourselves and about God. This book is an invitation to embark on that journey, contemplating the cosmos through faith, with hope, responsibility, and a profound sense of wonder.

The Universe as Creation

In the contemplation of the cosmos through the lens of faith, we find ourselves at the precipice of an expansive dialogue between science and spirituality. It's in the vast expanse of the universe that one can truly see the fingerprints of the Almighty, a sentiment echoing the essence of Catholic teaching and cosmological discovery. The universe, in its boundless grandeur and complex design, serves not merely as a backdrop to our existence but as a testament to the omnipotence and providence of God. This chapter endeavors to bridge the understanding of the universe as creation, exploring the intricate relationship between Catholic teaching, cosmology, and the inherent signs of God's grandeur woven into the fabric of existence.

The narrative of creation, as presented in the scriptures, offers a foundational perspective on the universe's origin and purpose. It's a narrative that finds resonance not only in the heart of the faithful but also in the curious mind of the scientist. The intention here is to not delimit the scientific exploration but to broaden the understanding of creation beyond the confines of observable phenomena, integrating the presence and action of a divine Creator.

Within the Catholic tradition, the doctrine of creation out of nothing (creatio ex nihilo) establishes God as the ultimate source of all that exists. It's a principle that complements scientific discovery by attributing the inception of the physical universe to a cause beyond physical dimensions and laws. This understanding encourages a profound respect for the universe, seen as a deliberate act of a caring Creator, rather than a mere accident of physics.

The concept of providence plays a crucial role in Catholic teaching, emphasizing God's ongoing involvement in creation. It's a theological premise that doesn't contradict the laws of nature but elevates them to reflect the order and purpose instilled by God. The intricacies and laws governing the cosmos are perceived not as chains of deterministic events but as expressions of divine will, guiding the universe towards its ultimate fulfillment.

The exploration of space and the pursuit of making humans a multiplanetary species carry both challenges and opportunities for faith. They compel us to reconsider our place in the universe and God's plan for humanity. This journey into the unknown is not devoid of spiritual meaning but is imbued with a sense of participation in the unfolding of creation's story. The endeavor to expand beyond our terrestrial confines, while ambitious, prompts a reflection on our responsibility as stewards of the universe, a concept deeply rooted in Catholic social teachings.

As humanity stands on the cusp of interstellar exploration, it's imperative to approach this frontier with both humility and hope. The vastness of space, with its countless galaxies and potential worlds, offers a humbling reminder of our smallness in the grand scheme of creation. Yet, it also magnifies the greatness of God, whose creative power is boundless and benevolent. This cosmic perspective invites a deeper appreciation for the mystery of existence and the intricate balance of life.

The dialogue between science and faith, particularly in the context of cosmology, enriches our understanding of the universe as creation. It's a dialogue that transcends the empirical confines of science, reaching into the realm of meaning and purpose. The Catholic tradition, with its long history of engaging with the sciences, provides a rich framework for this conversation, embracing the discoveries of cosmology while reflecting on their implications for faith and human understanding.

In our quest for knowledge and exploration of the universe, we are guided not only by scientific curiosity but also by a moral imperative. The stewardship of the universe, as entrusted to humanity by God, demands a conscientious approach to exploration and utilization of cosmic resources. It's a stewardship grounded in gratitude, reverence, and a commitment to the common good, principles that align with the Catholic vision of creation.

The universe, in its unfathomable vastness and beauty, serves as a canvas for God's creative genius. Each star, planet, and galaxy reveals aspects of God's nature - His creativity, power, and love for diversity. The beauty of the cosmos, from the macroscopic scale of galaxies to the microscopic world of quantum particles, reflects the beauty of the Creator, inviting us to a deeper relationship with God through the contemplation of His creation.

The pursuit of making humans a multiplanetary species, while a testament to our technological prowess, also invites reflection on the spiritual dimensions of this endeavor. It's an undertaking that requires not only ingenuity and resilience but also an acknowledgment of our dependence on God's providence. The challenges and uncertainties of space exploration remind us of our need for divine guidance and the importance of seeking God's will in our ambitions.

In conclusion, the universe as creation encapsulates a profound truth about our existence and purpose. It's a truth that bridges the realms of science and faith, inviting us to see the hand of God in the fabric of the cosmos. As we explore the mysteries of the universe, let us do so with a sense of wonder, responsibility, and reliance on divine providence, mindful of our role as stewards and co-creators in this magnificent creation.

The journey through space and time, from the moment of creation to the present and into the future, is a journey that we undertake not in isolation but in communion with the Creator. It's a journey that calls us to explore, to steward, and to marvel at the universe, recognizing in it the signature of the divine. This chapter has sought to illuminate the universe as creation, inviting a dialogue between cosmology and Catholic teaching that reveals the grandeur of God and the sacredness of the cosmos.

As we continue to contemplate the cosmos through the lens of faith, let us remain open to the insights of science, the wisdom of theology, and the guiding light of divine providence. The universe, in all its complexity and beauty, stands as a testament to the almighty Creator, inviting us to explore, understand, and cherish it as an expression of God's continuous act of creation.

Understanding Cosmology and Catholic Teaching

The endeavor to comprehend the cosmos has been a significant part of human curiosity since time immemorial. The Catholic Church's teachings provide a rich perspective on this quest, asserting that the universe is a creation of God, imbued with order and purpose. This section delves into the nexus between cosmology—the study of the universe in its totality—and Catholic teaching, exploring how faith and reason are not antagonistic but complementary paths to truth.

Catholic teaching posits that the universe, in its vast expanse and intricate laws, reflects the grandeur and intelligence of its Creator. From the majestic spiral galaxies to the minutiae of quantum mechanics, every aspect of the cosmos is seen as a signpost to the divine. This perspective invites believers and scientists alike to approach the study of the universe with a sense of wonder and a quest for deeper understanding.

Modern cosmology presents a universe that is ever-expanding, with galaxies moving away from each other in the fabric of space-time. This dynamic view of the cosmos can evoke a sense of awe that resonates with the Catholic understanding of a creation that is alive with the glory of God. The Church recognizes the Big Bang theory not as a challenge to the doctrine of creation, but as a scientific model that aligns with the belief in a temporal beginning of the universe, consonant with Genesis.

The principle of providence is central to Catholic teaching, asserting that God governs the creatures of the universe with wisdom and love. In the context of cosmology, this suggests that the laws of physics and the unfolding of cosmic events are underpinned by divine providence. God's presence is not confined to the miraculous but permeates the ordinary workings of the natural world, guiding the cosmic dance of matter and energy.

Catholics hold that human beings bear the imago Dei, the image of God, endowing them with a unique capacity for reason and moral reflection. This anthropology has significant implications for cosmology and space exploration. It suggests that humans have a role as stewards of the universe, called to study and care for it, recognizing the intrinsic value of creation while pursuing scientific advancement.

Space exploration, from this vantage point, is not just a technological achievement but a spiritual journey that reflects humanity's God-given curiosity and desire to explore the mysteries of creation. The possibility of becoming a multiplanetary species carries not only scientific implications but also theological ones, inviting reflections on the nature of salvation, the universality of Christ's redemption, and the inclusive reach of God's love.

Against this backdrop, Catholic teaching on the universe as creation fosters a dialogue between faith and science, encouraging a holistic understanding that embraces scientific discovery while rooted in spiritual truth. The Church supports the exploration of the cosmos as a way to marvel at the greatness of God's creation, urging that such endeavors be pursued with ethical considerations that respect the integrity of creation and promote the common good.

An informed Catholic cosmology, therefore, appreciates the scientific quest to understand the universe while discerning its spiritual significance. This integration of knowledge and faith reflects the Catholic tradition's long-standing engagement with science, from the contributions of clerical astronomers in the Vatican Observatory to the Church's dialogue with contemporary cosmologists.

The ethical dimensions of cosmology and space exploration are critically important. As humanity extends its reach into the cosmos, Catholic teaching calls for respect for the cosmic order and the responsible stewardship of space as God's creation. The Church's social teachings, with their emphasis on the dignity of life and the preferential option for the poor, offer guiding principles for ensuring that space exploration serves humanity's holistic development, avoiding the exploitation of cosmic resources for the benefit of a few.

In grappling with the complexities of the universe, Catholics are invited to perceive creation as a sacramental reality, where the material world points beyond itself to the transcendent. This sacramental vision enriches the scientific endeavor, opening up avenues for perceiving the interconnectedness of all things in the light of divine grace.

The future of cosmology and space exploration is fraught with both promise and peril. Catholic teaching, with its dual commitment to the pursuit of truth and the promotion of human dignity, offers a framework for navigating these challenges. By fostering a culture of dialogue between faith and science, the Church contributes to a cosmology that not only seeks to understand the universe but also to discern its meaning within the context of God's providential plan.

As the boundaries of human knowledge expand to include more of the cosmos, the Church remains a companion in the journey, encouraging scientists and believers to approach the universe with humility, gratitude, and a deep sense of purpose. The Catholic vision of the cosmos as creation serves not only to deepen our understanding of the universe but also to inspire a renewed appreciation for the Creator who brought it into being and sustains it in love.

In this light, understanding cosmology and Catholic teaching together unfolds as an invitation to an integrated exploration of reality, where the mysteries of the cosmos and the mysteries of faith converge, leading us to a fuller appreciation of our place in the universe and our relationship with the Creator. This holistic approach underscores the belief that scientific inquiry and religious faith are not isolated endeavors but are interrelated aspects of the human quest for truth and meaning.

The study of the cosmos, therefore, is not just an academic pursuit but a spiritual adventure, calling us to look beyond the surface of things to the deeper realities they signify. In this journey, the Catholic tradition provides a compass, guiding us to contemplate the universe not merely as a vast space of physical phenomena but as a sacred creation, a testament to the boundless creativity and love of God.

The Universe: Signs of God's Grandeur

As we traverse from the foundational understanding of the cosmos within a theological context, we delve into the realm where faith and science converge, revealing the breathtaking expanse of God's creation. The universe, with its sheer vastness and intricate design, stands as a testament to the grandeur of God. It prompts us to reflect on the divine artistry woven into the fabric of existence. This exploration, both scientific and spiritual, beckons us to contemplate the Creator's omnipotence and providential care through the lens of the cosmos.

The cosmic ballet of planets, stars, and galaxies, as observed by telescopes and spacecraft, speaks volumes of a universe governed by laws that are both precise and purposeful. Science has unveiled the intricate order and fine-tuning necessary for life to exist, pointing towards a grand design. From the fundamental forces that hold atoms together to the complex mechanisms driving galaxies, every aspect of the universe reveals a harmony that can be seen as a reflection of divine wisdom.

The endeavor of space exploration, a human pursuit marked by both curiosity and ambition, aligns with the innate desire to understand our place in this vast universe. As we reach for the stars, seeking to become a multiplanetary species, this quest is not merely a scientific venture but a spiritual journey. It is a pursuit that mirrors our longing to grasp the full extent of God's creation, to witness firsthand the breadth of His grandeur manifested across the cosmos.

The possibility of human life thriving on other planets or moons within our solar system or beyond presents a profound opportunity to witness God's providence in action. The Catholic teaching embraces this exploration as a means to glorify God by uncovering the magnificence of His creation. The expansion into space serves not only as a testament to human ingenuity but as a celebration of the Creator's boundless generosity in bestowing upon us a universe rich with wonders yet to be discovered.

As we ponder the universe, its origin, and its unfolding destiny, we are reminded of the divine attribute of providence. God, in His wisdom, created the universe ex nihilo, out of nothing, setting forth a cosmic narrative that science seeks to understand. This narrative, when viewed through the lens of faith, reveals a story of love, purpose, and hope. It tells us that the universe, in all its complexity, is not the product of random chance but the deliberate act of a loving Creator.

The exploration of space, then, becomes an act of faith, a declaration of trust in God's providence. It is an acknowledgment that, as we venture beyond our earthly confines, we are guided by the divine hand that has orchestrated the cosmos from the beginning. This journey is imbued with a sense of divine purpose, a call to explore the heavens not as a means of escaping our responsibilities on Earth, but as a way of drawing closer to God, understanding His creation, and fulfilling our role within it.

Moreover, the Catholic perspective on the universe and space exploration underscores the inherent value of all creation. Just as every star in the sky and every planet in its orbit reflects the glory of God, so too does every endeavor to reach beyond our current limitations. Each step taken towards understanding the cosmos is a step towards understanding the Creator, a journey that enriches our faith and deepens our awe for the divine majesty that pervades the universe.

In this grand cosmic scheme, humanity holds a special place. Made in the image and likeness of God, humans are called to stewardship of creation, entrusted with the care of Earth and the exploration of the heavens. This stewardship is a sacred duty, a way of honoring God by cherishing and protecting the work of His hands. As stewards, we are invited to see the universe not as a resource to be exploited, but as a gift to be treasured, a reflection of God's love and creativity.

The quest for knowledge, therefore, is not merely an academic or technical pursuit but a spiritual endeavor. It is an expression of our desire to know God more intimately and to participate in His creative work. Through the study of the cosmos, we engage in a dialogue with the Creator, seeking to uncover the mysteries of the universe as a means of drawing closer to the source of all being.

In conclusion, the universe, in its infinite complexity and beauty, stands as a sign of God's grandeur. It is a canvas upon which the story of creation is artfully depicted, inviting humanity to explore, to wonder, and to worship. As we continue to push the boundaries of space exploration and strive to become a multiplanetary species, we do so with the knowledge that we are part of a larger cosmic narrative. This narrative, guided by divine providence, calls us to see the universe as a testament to God's almighty power and to find our place within His magnificent creation.

Therefore, as we look up at the night sky, let us remember that each star, each planet, each galaxy is a sign of God's love for us. They beckon us to embark on a journey not just through space but through faith, a journey that leads us closer to the heart of the Creator. The universe, with all its mysteries and marvels, is an open invitation to discover the depth of God's grandeur and to take our rightful place in the ongoing story of creation.

"For from him and through him and for him are all things. To him be glory forever. Amen." (Romans 11:36)

Chapter 2: God, the First Cause and Final End

As we delve into the understanding of the universe, it is imperative to grasp its origin and destiny. In the realm of existence, it's not the chains of events that most captivate the contemplative mind but the uncaused Cause, the Prime Mover unmoved, the Supreme Architect of all that is seen and unseen. God, classically understood as the First Cause, is preeminent not only in initiating the cosmos but also as its Final End, the telos toward which all of creation inevitably moves.

Cosmological inquiries reveal a universe expanding from a single point, suggesting that space, time, and matter have a finite beginning. Astute observers of the cosmos can't help but ponder the source from whence came the singularity that science posits. Intriguingly, theology and philosophy converge on the concept of a necessary being, one whose essence entails existence and thus cannot not exist. This being is identified with God, who is the First Cause of all that exists (Catechism of the Catholic Church, 1994).

It's in the grandeur of the heavens where one discerns not merely the vastness of space but also the signature of a Divine Artist. The elegance of cosmic laws, the fine-tuning of universal constants, and the harmony of celestial spheres resonate with a symphonic testament to a Creator's intelligence and benevolence. For every law discovered and every particle observed bear the indelible mark of intention and design.

Revelation confirms what reason intimates. Genesis speaks of a beginning orchestrated by God, "In the beginning, God created the heavens and the earth" (Genesis 1:1). This ancient text, while not a scientific account, encapsulates profound truths resonating with the findings of modern astronomy. The beginning surmised by cosmologists echoes the primordial genesis heralded by scripture. Therefore, interpreting the text within the context of current cosmological insights reflects a synthesis of faith and reason, both guided by Divine Providence.

Providence, understood as God's ongoing participation in the world, directs and sustains the cosmos toward its intended purposes. Not a deistic watchmaker who winds up the universe and steps away, but rather a sustainer engaged in each instant, ensuring the cooperative dance of natural laws and chance events weaves into the tapestry of a meaningful history.

It's within this providential guidance that space exploration finds its significance and moral gravity. Human efforts to become a multiplanetary species are not outside the purview of Divine Providence but can be seen as participating in the creative and exploratory impulses ingrained in our very being.

Exploration is a testament to the inquisitiveness and innovation endowed unto humanity, reflecting the Creator's ingenuity.

Despite our advancements, our sun and even our galaxy are but minuscule fractions of the entire cosmos. Yet, our solar-centric perspectives must broaden in recognition that the universe's unfolding is oriented toward a Final End beyond mere physical processes. This cosmic telos is not bound by entropy nor the heat death of stars but is anchored in the immutable and eternal nature of God.

God's omniscience can't be overstated. The Divine Mind, which knows every possibility and actuality, orchestrates a grand cosmic narrative, encompassing the entirety of time and space. Every celestial body, from the mightiest quasar to the humblest asteroid, possesses a place in creation's grand design.

As humanity ventures forth, buoyed by advancements in cosmology and technology, it's pivotal to remember that our destinies aren't confined to the material. The finality of our cosmic journey finds its meaning not in the stars we reach but in attaining the union with the transcendent source from which all being flows. The beatific vision remains the ultimate horizon.

The universe's complexity and expanse may seem to obscure God's presence, yet paradoxically, it also heightens His closeness. Every quantum leap and cosmic vista expands the human spirit, beckoning it toward a greater comprehension of the Creator. As such, creation does not distract from God but magnificently points towards Him, inviting a deeper exploration of the Divine Mystery.

Moreover, the natural order's beauty and grandeur serve as a constant invitation to seek the First Cause amidst the cosmos's expanse. Each discovery, rather than diminishing the Creator's role, magnifies the splendor of His works. For in the vastness of space, the fingerprints of God's artistry invite wonder and worship.

Thus, the narrative of humankind becoming an interstellar species is intrinsically theological. It's an act faithful to our calling as co-creators, stewards of the cosmos, invited to share in the divine creativity that birthed the stars. Our odyssey among the heavens is not only a physical endeavor but a spiritual pilgrimage towards an encounter with the Infinite.

To apprehend God as the First Cause and Final End is to realize that all endeavors, be they scientific or theological, are enfolded within the divine Logos. The universe's intelligibility speaks of the Logos, inviting us to participate in the divine life spiraling through creation, drawing all things toward the Omega Point where God awaits.

When considering space exploration and its profound implications, it becomes evident that humanity's reach for the stars is intricately woven into a providential plan. Our quest is not an escape from divine reality but a deeper penetration into the mystery enveloping and sustaining the universe. Recognizing God's role as both origin and goal offers a comprehensive vision that harmonizes the pursuits of cosmology with the enduring wisdom of Catholic thought.

In the final analysis, the quest for the stars is inextricably linked with the quest for God. The drive to explore and inhabit new worlds and the quest for the Ultimate Reality are pursuits that reflect our unique human vocation—a vocation to seek, to find, and ultimately to reside with God, the Alpha and Omega, the First Cause and Final End of all that exists.

Genesis, Cosmology, and the Catholic Perspective

In pursuing an understanding of the cosmos from a Catholic viewpoint, it is essential to navigate the realms of Genesis, cosmology, and the Catholic perspective intertwined. The Genesis account of creation provides a foundational narrative for Christians, illustrating God's omnipotence and the intrinsic goodness of creation. However, in an age where cosmology advances our comprehension of the universe at an unprecedented rate, a dialogue between faith and science becomes indispensable. This chapter endeavors to explore this dialogue, emphasizing God's role as both the First Cause and the Final End within the context of modern cosmology and space exploration.

The Catholic Church teaches that faith and reason are complementary, not contradictory (Catechism of the Catholic Church, 1997). When examining the universe, both science and faith contribute to a fuller understanding of reality. Cosmology, the scientific study of the universe's origin, structure, and ultimate fate, has offered remarkable insights into the cosmos that were unimaginable in previous centuries. While scientific methods reveal the universe's immense age and the vast expanse of space, Catholic theology provides a framework for understanding the purpose and significance of creation in relation to God.

The narrative of Genesis, when interpreted through the lens of Catholic teaching, does not stand in opposition to scientific accounts of the universe's origins but rather complements them. The Church posits that the story of Genesis is not a scientific account but a theological and philosophical text meant to communicate profound truths about God, humanity, and creation (Pontifical Biblical Commission, 1993). This interpretation encourages believers to see God's hand in the formation of the universe, not through the specifics of how it was made, but in the existence and order of creation itself.

Within this framework, the Big Bang theory, which posits that the universe began as a singular, infinitely dense point before expanding, can be seen as a moment of creation that aligns with the belief in God as the First Cause. The remarkable fine-tuning of the universe, which allows for the possibility of life, can, from a Catholic perspective, be seen as evidence of providential design—an indication of a universe created with purpose and intent.

As humanity extends its reach into space, exploring planets and stars far beyond our own, this endeavor too finds a place within Catholic thought. The exploration of the heavens is not merely a scientific or technological achievement but an act of engaging with the majesty and complexity of God's creation. It invites a sense of wonder and awe, which are deeply spiritual responses to the natural world, and encourages a reflective consideration of humanity's place in the universe.

Providence, a key aspect of Catholic theology, emphasizes God's ongoing involvement in creation. In the vast, unfolding cosmos, providence assures believers that nothing escapes God's care and attention, not even the furthest galaxies. This belief in providential care challenges the notion of an indifferent universe, proposing instead that creation is sustained and held in being by God's will.

Furthermore, the Catholic perspective sees humanity's role in the cosmos as stewards of God's creation. This stewardship is not limited to the Earth but extends to how humans interact with the cosmos at large. Ethical considerations in space exploration, such as respecting the integrity of other planets and avoiding the exploitation of extraterrestrial resources, are informed by this understanding of stewardship.

The finality of creation, or its orientation towards a final end, is another aspect where Catholic thought intersects with cosmology. The eschatological belief that creation moves towards a culmination in God gives cosmic history a meaningful directionality. This perspective imbues the scientific study of the universe's ultimate fate—whether it be in heat death, a big crunch, or some other scenario—with a theological significance.

It suggests that the physical end of the cosmos is not its ultimate end, but rather its transformation and fulfillment in God.

In light of space exploration's capability to profoundly alter humanity's understanding of itself and its place in the universe, Catholic teaching offers principles for guiding this endeavor. By framing the quest to become a multiplanetary species within the context of God's creation, the Church provides a moral and ethical compass for navigating the challenges and opportunities that lie ahead.

In conclusion, the Catholic perspective on Genesis, cosmology, and the role of God as the First Cause and Final End provides a comprehensive framework for understanding the cosmos. It bridges faith and reason, showing that scientific discovery and theological reflection can coexist and enrich each other. As humans venture further into the cosmos, this dialogue between the Church and the scientific community will continue to evolve, illuminating new facets of the mystery of creation and the Creator.

Interpreting Genesis in the Age of Space Exploration As humanity extends its reach into the cosmos, the intersection between divine providence and space exploration becomes increasingly nuanced. The Book of Genesis, with its poetic account of creation, offers profound insights, even as we propel human technology beyond Earth's atmosphere. This section explores how the timeless teachings of Genesis can inform and inspire the Catholic faithful and the broader scientific community in this new era of cosmic discovery.

The narrative of Genesis presents a universe meticulously crafted by God, imbued with purpose and order. It's a vision that resonates with the awe and wonder many feel when gazing at the night sky or witnessing images beamed back from the far reaches of space. The vastness of the universe, rather than diminishing the biblical account, magnifies the Creator's grandeur—an assertion that aligns with Catholic teaching and finds renewed relevance in the context of space exploration.

Space exploration challenges us to reconcile our understanding of this grand universe with the scriptural depiction of creation. Genesis, in the age of space exploration, becomes not a historical or scientific text but a theological compass guiding us through the moral and spiritual implications of extending human presence into the heavens. It reaffirms God as the first cause and final end, a truth that remains steadfast whether one stands on the surface of Earth or the soil of a distant planet.

As cosmonauts and astronauts traverse the heavens, the doctrine of divine providence reminds us that God's governance encompasses all creation. This providential care extends beyond the bounds of Earth, inviting humans to see space as a domain of God's unfolding plan for the universe. In our exploration and study of space, we participate in the divine act of creation, uncovering the wonders God has wrought. It's a participation that calls for humility and responsibility, recognizing our role as stewards rather than conquerors of the cosmos.

The Catholic understanding of creation, as articulated through Genesis, speaks to the intrinsic goodness of the universe. Every star, planet, and galaxy, every phenomenon from the smallest quantum particle to vast interstellar clouds, is a testament to God's creative love. This perspective invites a sense of reverence in the study and exploration of space, urging scientists and believers alike to approach the cosmos not merely as a resource to be exploited but as a sacred trust to be preserved.

In this light, the efforts to make humanity a multiplanetary species take on a profound theological dimension. The endeavor to inhabit other worlds is seen not just as a technological milestone but as a continuation of the divine command to "fill the earth and subdue it" (Genesis 1:28), expanded now to the broader canvas of creation. Such a view challenges us to integrate space exploration within a framework of care, ensuring that our cosmic journeys reflect the respect and love due to all of God's creation.

The ethical imperatives outlined in Genesis provide a moral foundation as we reach beyond our planet. The mandate to steward the Earth is amplified in the context of space, where the fragility of life and the interconnectedness of creation become unmistakably clear. This stewardship demands a commitment to peace, sustainability, and the common good, principles that must guide our actions whether on Earth or amongst the stars.

The unity of the human family, a central theme in Genesis, also informs our approach to space exploration. Just as Genesis depicts humanity as created in the image of God, so too does it remind us of our shared dignity and destiny. The collaborative nature of space missions, which brings together people from diverse nations and backgrounds, can be seen as a reflection of this biblical ideal, pointing towards a future where the exploration of space unites humanity in a common purpose.

In pursuing the cosmos, we are also reminded of the limits of human ambition. Genesis speaks to the need for humility before the mysteries of creation, a lesson that resonates deeply in the age of space exploration. The challenges and risks associated with venturing into space underscore our dependence on divine providence and the need for prudence, reminding us that while we are co-creators with God, we are not the ultimate masters of the universe.

Finally, the exploration of space deepens our appreciation for the mystery of creation. Just as Genesis opens with the words "In the beginning, God created the heavens and the earth," so does each new discovery in the cosmos invite us to ponder the origins and purpose of the universe. This sense of wonder and curiosity is a gift, leading us closer to the Creator and inspiring a continuous search for understanding in the vast expanse of space.

In conclusion, interpreting Genesis in the age of space exploration enriches our understanding of both scripture and the cosmos. It invites a dialogue between faith and science, where each can inform and illuminate the other. As we stand on the threshold of new cosmic frontiers, let us carry forward the wisdom of Genesis, seeing in our spacefaring endeavors a reflection of the divine image and a participation in the ongoing story of creation.

The Ethical Imperatives of Exploring the Heavens

In the panorama of human exploration, the venture into the cosmos stands as a testament to not only our technological advancements but also our relentless spirit of inquiry. As stewards of Earth and everything within it, as bestowed by the Divine Providence, embarking upon the cosmic sea calls for a reflection of our ethical frameworks, particularly under the guidance of Catholic teachings. The exploration of the heavens, while a symbol of human achievement, also posits significant ethical considerations that must be navigated with prudence and respect for creation.

The morality of reaching beyond Earth lies at the heart of our cosmic journey. Venturing into space must not be seen solely as an opportunity for human aggrandizement or a mere extension of Earth's geopolitical rivalries. Instead, it is an invitation to contemplate the vastness of God's creation and our place within it. This celestial endeavor bears the potential to enrich our understanding of the universe, fostering an appreciation for the intricacies of God's handywork. However, it also necessitates a mindful approach, ensuring that our actions in space promote the common good and reflect our responsibilities as custodians of creation.

Such stewardship of the universe, viewed through the lens of Catholic duty, demands an ethically grounded approach to space exploration. The principles of justice, peace, and the integrity of creation must guide our steps into the cosmic domain. The exploitation of celestial bodies for commercial or militaristic purposes stands in stark contrast to the vocation of stewardship that calls for the protection and reverence of creation. Responsible exploration, thus, requires adhering to a framework that respects the intrinsic value of the cosmos as part of God's grand design.

The silent majesty of space, with its infinite galaxies and stars, beckons us not only to explore but to wonder at the majesty of the Creator. Such exploration, inherently imbued with both risk and opportunity, challenges us to extend the boundaries of our moral and ethical considerations. The possibility of encountering extraterrestrial life forms or habitable worlds adds a profound dimension to our cosmic journey, compelling us to ponder the universality of God's grace and the potential for a broader cosmic fraternity.

Within this context, the Catholic Church's teachings offer a foundational ethos for engaging with the cosmos. The respect for life, the pursuit of peace, and the commitment to universal fraternity are pillars that should illuminate our space endeavors. These principles underscore the need for a cooperative approach to space exploration, where the fruits of scientific discoveries are shared equitably, benefiting all humankind and reflecting the interconnectedness of God's creation.

As we venture beyond the confines of our planet, the principle of the common good serves as a critical guide. Space, a domain of all humanity, must not become the preserve of the wealthy or the powerful. The equitable distribution of space's potential benefits, with a particular emphasis on assisting those most in need, mirrors the Gospel's call to love and serve our neighbors. This ethos of inclusivity and solidarity is paramount in ensuring that space exploration contributes to the well-being of the entire human family.

The ethical imperatives of exploring the heavens also demand attention to the fragility of our own planet. The awe-inspiring images of Earth from space, a delicate blue orb cradled in the dark infinity, serve as a poignant reminder of the vulnerability of our home. Thus, our forays into the cosmos should reinforce rather than undermine our resolve to address the pressing environmental challenges facing our planet. The stewardship of Earth, our primary garden in the vast universe, remains an indispensable duty, even as we gaze into the stars.

The pursuit of knowledge, a noble endeavor sanctioned by the Catholic faith, finds profound expression in space exploration.

Yet, this quest must be tethered to humility and a recognition of the limits of human understanding and control. The vastness of the universe, a testament to the omnipotence of God, reminds us of our finite nature and the ultimate reliance on Divine Providence. We explore, not to conquer or dominate, but to learn, appreciate, and better steward the gifts entrusted to us.

In navigating the ethical terrain of space exploration, the concept of universal destination of goods remains a guiding star. This principle, deeply rooted in Catholic social teaching, underscores that the goods of the Earth—and, by extension, the cosmos—are intended by God for the benefit of all humanity. Thus, our endeavors in space must be marked by a generosity of spirit, ensuring that advances in space science and technology contribute to the alleviation of suffering and the promotion of human dignity on Earth.

As humanity stands on the threshold of becoming a multiplanetary species, our ethical considerations must evolve to encompass not only the residents of Earth but also the potentiality of life beyond our planet. The sacredness of life, in all its forms, demands a respect that transcends the boundaries of our world. Our encounters with the unknown in the cosmos should be approached with a posture of reverence and a commitment to peace, embodying the Catholic ethos of encountering the "other" with love and respect.

In sum, the exploration of the heavens beckons us to a higher calling—a journey not just across the physical universe but also into the depths of our moral and spiritual convictions. As we reach for the stars, let us do so with hearts anchored in the wisdom of our faith, ensuring that our celestial endeavors honor the Creator, promote the common good, and reflect the inherent dignity of all creation. The heavens, in their splendor, invite us not to dominion but to stewardship, to wonder, and to an ever-deeper understanding of our place in the cosmos under the gaze of God's providential care.

Let the venture into the vastness of space be a testament to human solidarity, our shared guardianship of creation, and our collective pursuit of knowledge imbued with ethical integrity. In this way, the exploration of the heavens can become a luminous path leading us closer to the Divine, revealing the intricate tapestry of creation interwoven with the threads of love, justice, and peace. As we embark on this cosmic journey, may our efforts be a harmonious symphony to the glory of the Creator, whose handiwork is declared by the heavens themselves.

The Morality of Reaching Beyond Earth

As humanity stands on the brink of becoming a multiplanetary species, a profound inquiry into the morality of reaching beyond Earth is not only timely but essential. This task requires an exploration of ethical imperatives through the lens of Catholic teachings, juxtaposed with the advancements of cosmic exploration. In doing so, it becomes apparent that the venture into the heavens is not merely a physical journey but a moral and spiritual odyssey that reflects our deepest values and responsibilities.

The ambition to explore and perhaps colonize celestial bodies brings to the fore a constellation of moral concerns. At the heart of these is the principle of stewardship, a concept deeply embedded in Catholic doctrine. Stewardship calls us to respect and care for all of creation as a reflection of God's grandeur. This duty extends beyond the confines of our planet, urging us to consider the cosmos as a sacred trust. In navigating the heavens, humanity must thus carry the mantle of stewards, ensuring that our cosmic endeavors honor the Creator by preserving the inherent value of the universe.

Integral to the discussion of extraterrestrial exploration is the principle of the common good. Viewed through a Catholic prism, the pursuit of knowledge and expansion into space must serve humanity as a whole. This belief challenges endeavors motivated by profit or national pride, instead advocating for initiatives that improve human understanding, foster peace, and contribute to the well-being of all Earth's inhabitants. The common good, therefore, becomes a compass guiding the ethics of space exploration, ensuring that our reach into the heavens promotes solidarity and respect among all people.

The exploration of space also poses the question of encountering other forms of life. While speculative at present, the possibility invites us to reflect on our moral obligations to any extraterrestrial beings we might discover. Catholic teaching, with its emphasis on the dignity of all creation, suggests a posture of respect, curiosity, and non-interference. Such an approach not only aligns with the concept of stewardship but also with the recognition of the vast and mysterious Intelligence behind the universe. Engaging with other life forms, should they exist, must be approached with humility and an openness to the broader manifestations of divine creativity.

Moreover, the venture into space renews the imperative to care for our own planet. The striking images of Earth from space have reinforced our planet's fragility and the interconnectedness of all life. From a Catholic perspective, the desire to explore the heavens should not distract from our responsibilities to Earth but rather deepen our commitment to its stewardship. The moral and ethical considerations of space exploration, therefore, encompass a call to renewed ecological consciousness and action.

Yet, as we contemplate reaching beyond Earth, we are faced with the limitations of our own understanding and capabilities. The principle of prudence, a virtue extolled in Catholic ethics, requires a careful assessment of the risks and uncertainties associated with space exploration. This involves a judicious evaluation of the potential consequences, both foreseen and unforeseen, ensuring that our cosmic ambitions do not lead to harm or irreversible damage. The wisdom of prudence calls for a balanced approach, one that weighs the excitement of discovery against the solemn responsibilities we bear.

The moral contours of extending human presence into the cosmos are further shaped by the concept of Providence. Catholic theology upholds the belief in God's ongoing guidance and care for creation. In the context of space exploration, this conviction invites trust in divine Providence while emphasizing human cooperation with God's purposes. Our endeavors in the heavens, then, must be pursued with an awareness of our partnership with the Creator, seeking not to conquer or dominate but to participate humbly in the unfolding of the cosmic story.

In conclusion, the morality of reaching beyond Earth encompasses a tapestry of ethical considerations, illuminated by the light of Catholic teaching. Our journey to the stars is inscribed with questions of stewardship, the common good, respect for potential extraterrestrial life, ecological responsibility, prudence, and Providence. As humanity aspires to inhabit the heavens, we are called to act with wisdom, integrity, and a profound sense of our place within God's creation. Let our exploration of the cosmos be a testament to our commitment to these values, guiding us to tread gently across the heavens as faithful stewards of the divine mystery that envelops us.

Stewardship of the Universe: A Catholic Duty Moving forward from understanding the universe as a creation and God as its architect, it's vital to discuss the responsibilities that come with these truths. The Catholic tradition, deeply embedded with teachings on stewardship, extends its principles to the vastness of the cosmos. The duty of stewardship, traditionally applied to Earth's environment and resources, naturally expands to encompass the entire universe in the context of modern space exploration.

At the heart of Catholic teaching is the belief that creation is an expression of God's love and power. Every star, planet, and galactic phenomenon reveals something of God's nature (Catechism of the Catholic Church, 1992). As humans, created in the image of God, we're endowed with the responsibility to care for and respect all creation. This responsibility doesn't end at the Kármán line but stretches infinitely into the cosmos.

The principle of stewardship in the Catholic tradition calls for a respectful, caring, and prudent use of creation. This principle isn't just for the things we see around us—it also applies to the undiscovered and the unknown. Space, the final frontier, is part of the "garden" humanity is called to tend. As such, efforts to explore and possibly inhabit other worlds must be approached with a sense of duty to protect and preserve.

Exploring the heavens brings us face to face with the awe-inspiring complexity and beauty of God's creation. This exploration, however, must be guided by ethical imperatives that prioritize the well-being of the universe over human ambition. The prospect of becoming a multiplanetary species and expanding our horizons beyond Earth carries with it a profound responsibility to ensure that in our expansion, we do not mar the face of creation.

The Catholic understanding of Providence teaches that God is actively involved in the world, guiding and sustaining creation towards its ultimate good. This doctrine reminds us that our efforts in the cosmos are under Divine guidance. As we navigate the unknown, our actions must align with this providential care, acting as co-creators with God, not as usurpers or destroyers.

When considering the environmental ethics that have been discussed concerning Earth, similar principles apply to space. The environmental movement within the Church, highlighted by the encyclical Laudato Si' by Pope Francis, underscores the urgent need for an ecological conversion which appreciates creation's interconnectedness and intrinsic value. This ecological concern must also translate into how we engage with the cosmos, recognizing that celestial bodies are also part of God's creation and deserving of our respect.

The concept of the common good is central to Catholic social teaching. In the context of space exploration, this principle compels us to consider how our actions beyond Earth affect the entirety of humanity, including future generations. The cosmos is a shared heritage, a vast expanse that belongs to no single nation, person, or entity. As stewards, we're called to ensure that the benefits of space exploration are distributed justly and equitably, and that the pursuit of knowledge serves all of humanity.

As Catholics, we're invited to look beyond the immediate technical challenges of space exploration to the deeper questions it raises. What does it mean to be human in the vastness of space? How do we carry our values, ethics, and faith into this new frontier? The exploration of space isn't just a scientific or technological endeavor—it's a spiritual journey that invites us to reflect on our place in the universe and the Creator who made it all possible.

The dangers of exploitation in space, such as the depletion of celestial resources or the damage to extraterrestrial environments, are real concerns that need to be addressed from a standpoint of moral responsibility. Just as exploitation and environmental degradation on Earth are opposed by Catholic social teaching, similar actions in space fall under the same ethical scrutiny.

Human dignity, a cornerstone of Catholic ethics, must also be a guiding principle in the cosmos. As potential colonizers of other worlds, humans must guard against repeating historical errors of colonization that marginalized and oppressed. The dignity of any potential extraterrestrial life forms we encounter must also be respected, guided by a profound sense of humility and kinship with all of God's creation.

The pursuit of knowledge, central to the human experience, is a noble endeavor that reflects our imago Dei—the image of God within us. Our curiosity and desire to explore stem from this divine image. However, this pursuit must be tempered by wisdom and a keen awareness of our limitations. The vastness of the universe, coupled with its beauty and mystery, should draw us closer to the Creator, inspiring a sense of wonder and a desire to protect this grand cosmic tapestry.

As stewards of the universe, Catholics are called to lead by example, demonstrating that faith and science can coexist harmoniously. Our exploration of space should be marked by humility, respect for creation, and a commitment to the common good. By doing so, we not only honor the Creator but also contribute to the unfolding story of humanity in a way that uplifts and respects the sanctity of all creation.

In conclusion, the Catholic duty of stewardship extends beyond the confines of our planet to the farthest reaches of the universe. As we stand on the precipice of potentially monumental discoveries and achievements in space, our actions must reflect a deep-rooted commitment to ethical principles that uphold the dignity of creation, the pursuit of the common good, and the glorification of God through the careful and respectful exploration of His universe.

Our journey into the cosmos is not merely a series of scientific experiments or adventures; it is a spiritual voyage that asks us to bring our faith, ethics, and values along. Only by marrying these dimensions of our humanity with our scientific pursuits can we truly honor our calling as stewards of the universe—a duty that is both a privilege and a profound responsibility.

The Church's Role in the Age of Cosmic Exploration

In the quest to fathom the vistas of the cosmos, the Church finds itself at a juncture of faith and reason, theology and science. This chapter delves into how Catholicism, a faith deeply rooted in the contemplation of creation, engages with the modern odyssey of cosmic exploration. It's a dialogue that not only reflects upon the achievements of humanity in space but also contemplates the divine providence guiding this colossal journey.

The Church's engagement in the age of cosmic exploration is not just passive observation but an active dialogue with the scientific community. By embracing science, the Church continues its long-standing tradition of seeking understanding through the lens of faith. This dialogue fosters a unique perspective on space exploration, one that sees beyond the physical conquest of space to the spiritual and moral implications of these endeavors.

At the heart of Catholic teaching is the belief in God as the Creator of the universe. This foundational belief shapes the Church's response to cosmic exploration. The discoveries in space are not seen as mere advancements in human achievement but as deeper revelations of God's grandeur (Catechism of the Catholic Church, 1992). This perspective encourages a profound respect for the cosmos, not as a dominion to be conquered but as a creation to be revered and studied.

The role of the Church in this age goes beyond mere commentary; it involves moral guidance. As humanity reaches further into space, ethical questions of stewardship, exploitation, and the sanctity of life in the cosmos come to the forefront. The Church's teachings on the dignity of creation and the common good provide essential moral compasses guiding these ventures. These principles remind us that our exploration of the heavens must be undertaken with a sense of responsibility toward all of creation.

Pioneers of faith in the space era, such as Jesuit brother and scientist Guy Consolmagno, director of the Vatican Observatory, exemplify the Church's active participation in the dialogue between faith and science. Their work embodies the confluence of curiosity about the universe and a deep-seated faith in its Creator. This synergy between faith and science showcases the Church's support for discovering the truths of the cosmos, provided these pursuits are aligned with ethical and moral considerations.

The concept of Divine Providence plays a pivotal role in the Church's view of cosmic exploration. This belief posits that God's guiding hand is present in all of creation, including the vast expanse of space. This assurance inspires a hopeful outlook on space exploration, one that trusts in God's plan for the universe and humanity's role within it. It's a perspective that encourages exploration, tempered with humility and awe for the Creator's work.

This era of cosmic exploration presents unique opportunities for evangelization and dialogue. The Church's teachings can offer profound insights into the questions raised by our ventures into space. By engaging with scientists, astronauts, and cosmologists, the Church can provide spiritual and ethical perspectives that enrich the understanding of our place in the universe.

The pursuit of knowledge about the cosmos also resonates with the Catholic understanding of human reason and the quest for truth. The Church supports the scientific exploration of the universe as a means of further understanding God's creation. This endeavor, rooted in the awe of the cosmos, can be a profound act of worship, an acknowledgment of the Creator's magnificence (Pontifical Academy of Sciences, 2009).

However, as the Church navigates this dialogue, it also calls for caution against hubris and the dangers of exploiting the cosmos. The teachings on stewardship and the common good serve as reminders that our explorations should always respect the integrity of creation and seek to benefit all humanity, not just a privileged few.

In the context of making humans a multiplanetary species, the Church encourages a reflection on the theological implications of life beyond Earth. Such considerations extend the narrative of salvation history and the inclusivity of God's love to the whole cosmos. This speculative theology invites us to ponder our relationship with any potential extraterrestrial life forms and the universality of Christ's redemption.

The Church's role, then, is multifaceted. It acts as a moral compass, a partner in dialogue with science, and a source of spiritual reflection on the mysteries unveiled by cosmic exploration. This engagement is not without its challenges, as it navigates the complexities of integrating faith with the rapidly advancing frontiers of space science.

As humanity stands on the cusp of becoming an interplanetary species, the Church's teachings on the unity of creation, the dignity of life, and the primacy of love provide essential guidance. These principles help ensure that our journey into the cosmos is not just a technological feat but a step toward a fuller understanding of creation and our Creator.

In conclusion, the Church's role in the age of cosmic exploration is an embodiment of faith seeking understanding. It is a journey that embraces the unknown, guided by the light of faith, the pursuit of truth, and a commitment to the ethical dimensions of our cosmic endeavors. As we reach for the stars, the Church remains a steadfast companion, reminding us of the divine love that encompasses all of creation.

Catholicism and the Dialogue with Science

In the modern era, Catholicism's engagement with the scientific community, particularly in the realm of cosmology and space exploration, stands as a testament to the Church's adaptability and commitment to truth. The belief in an omnipotent Creator does not stand in opposition to scientific discovery; rather, it enriches the dialogue between faith and reason. The exploration of the cosmos does not diminish God's majesty but reveals the grandeur of His creation in more profound ways.

The Catholic Church, historically, has not only been a custodian of spiritual wisdom but also an avid supporter of the sciences. The Vatican Observatory, one of the oldest astronomical research institutions in the world, symbolizes this enduring commitment. This alignment demonstrates that the Church's interest lies not just within the spiritual realm but extends to understanding the physical universe as well.

This stance is firmly rooted in the understanding that truth is unified. The discoveries in the vastness of space are seen not as contradictions to Biblical narratives but as deeper revelations of the same truth. The narrative of creation, when interpreted through a lens that harmonizes faith and science, provides a richer understanding of the universe and our place within it.

Space exploration, in this context, is viewed as a noble endeavor. Venturing into the unknown, to understand more about our universe, is an act that mirrors the human longing for God. It stretches our capacities, both intellectually and spiritually, pushing us towards the outer limits of our understanding and beyond.

The dialogue between Catholicism and science, especially in the realm of cosmic exploration, is inherently philosophical. It raises questions about existence, purpose, and the finality of creation. These are not solely scientific questions but are deeply theological and existential as well. The Church contributes a perspective that grounds these explorations within the context of a creation that is purposeful and directed.

Providence plays a crucial role in this dialogue. The belief in a providential God reassures that the cosmos operates within a divine order. This understanding encourages a respectful approach to space exploration, one that recognizes cosmic events and entities not merely as subjects for human use but as part of a grander, divine orchestra.

However, the dialogue between Catholicism and science is not without its challenges. The rapid advancements in technology and the increasing capability for cosmic intervention raise ethical questions. These include concerns about the stewardship of outer space, the treatment of potential extraterrestrial life, and the moral implications of altering celestial bodies. Here, Catholic ethical principles provide a framework for responsible exploration and use of cosmic resources.

The Church also advocates for the inclusivity of the human family in the benefits derived from space exploration. This aligns with the Church's social teachings on the common good and the universal destination of goods. Space, viewed from this perspective, is a domain where scientific advancements should contribute to the well-being of all humanity, not just a privileged few.

In promoting dialogue with the scientific community, the Catholic Church emphasizes the importance of humility and openness. The recognition that human understanding is limited calls for a collaborative approach to exploration and study. It invites scientists and theologians alike to acknowledge the mystery that surrounds our existence and the cosmos.

The future of space exploration, as envisioned by the Church, is one that is guided by ethical considerations, inspired by a sense of wonder, and grounded in the pursuit of knowledge that serves the common good. It is a future where the vastness of the cosmos draws humanity closer together and closer to the Divine.

In conclusion, the dialogue between Catholicism and science, particularly in the age of cosmic exploration, is a dynamic and evolving conversation. It is characterized by mutual respect, a shared quest for truth, and a common awe in the face of the universe's wonders. This dialogue underscores the belief that the pursuit of scientific knowledge, when guided by ethical principles and open to transcendence, is a path that leads not away from God but towards a deeper understanding of His creation.

The Church's role in this age of cosmic exploration is not that of a bystander but as a participant that brings wisdom, ethical guidance, and a vision of unity. It challenges both the scientific community and the faithful to consider not just the how and what of creation but the why, inviting a holistic understanding of our universe that embraces both the seen and the unseen.

This dialogue between Catholicism and science enriches our approach to cosmic exploration, providing a framework that integrates faith and reason. It ensures that as we reach for the stars, we do so with both a sense of purpose and responsibility, mindful of our place within a creation that reflects the glory of its Creator.

Pioneers of Faith in the Space Era As we delve into the era of cosmic exploration, it is paramount to reflect on the figures who have seamlessly blended their steadfast faith with the relentless pursuit of understanding the universe. The journey into space, a domain vast and unknown, mirrors the spiritual journey of humanity towards understanding God's grandeur. This chapter aims to illuminate the lives and philosophical stances of individuals who have courageously stood at the intersection of faith and cosmic discovery.

The exploration of space, while a scientific endeavor, also manifests as a deeply spiritual quest. It requires a fortitude of spirit and an unwavering belief in something greater than oneself. Those at the forefront of this journey often find themselves grappling with questions that are as much theological in nature as they are scientific. How does the vastness of the universe align with the teachings of faith? Can the infinite depths of space bring us closer to understanding the Infinite Being?

Historically, members of the Catholic faith have played pivotal roles in the realms of astronomy and space exploration. This is not coincidental but a testament to the Catholic understanding of the universe as a creation of God, endowed with order and reason. It is this very perspective that fuels the curiosity of Catholic scientists, urging them to explore the cosmos not merely for discovery's sake but as a form of worship, seeking God through the marvels of His creation.

In the modern era, where the division between science and religion seems to widen, pioneers of faith in the space era remind us of the harmony that can exist between the two. They serve as beacons, demonstrating that the pursuit of scientific knowledge and the deepening of one's faith are not mutually exclusive but can, in fact, complement and enrich each other.

Consider the symbolic act by Astronaut Buzz Aldrin, a Presbyterian, who partook in communion on the surface of the moon. Though not Catholic, this act underscored the intrinsic human desire to connect profound human achievements and explorations with spiritual significance. It prompts us to ponder the potential of similar expressions of faith within the Catholic community, in the uncharted realms beyond our planet.

The silent and serene landscape of space provides a unique environment for contemplation and prayer. The vastness of the universe, with its billions of galaxies and stars, is a humbling reminder of our smallness in the grand scheme of God's creation. This realization, rather than diminishing our worth, magnifies the love of God who cares for each individual amidst the immensity.

Faithful explorers of the cosmos often speak of the overwhelming sense of awe and divine majesty experienced on witnessing the earth from space. This 'overview effect', a cognitive shift in awareness reported by some astronauts, aligns closely with the Catholic tradition of contemplative prayer, where one seeks to view oneself and the world from God's perspective. Through this lens, space exploration can be seen as a spiritual journey towards greater unity with the Creator.

The ethical considerations in exploring the heavens also resonate with Catholic teachings on stewardship of creation. The Catholic pioneers in space exploration advocate for responsible and equitable use of cosmic resources. They endeavor to ensure that the benefits of space exploration extend to all of humanity, reflecting the Catholic social teaching of the common good.

In dialogues regarding the potential colonization of other planets, the Catholic voice emphasizes the dignity of all creation and the need to approach such ventures with humility and respect. These discussions showcase the continued relevance of Catholic ethical principles in guiding humanity's steps into new worlds.

Moreover, the concept of cosmic citizenship, where Earthly inhabitants recognize their responsibility towards the greater cosmos, finds its roots in the Catholic understanding of universal brotherhood and interconnectedness of all God's creation. This perspective urges us to approach space exploration with a spirit of cooperation rather than domination, in service of the entire cosmic community.

As humanity stands on the brink of becoming a multiplanetary species, the insights and moral guidance rooted in Catholic tradition are invaluable. They ensure that as we reach outwards to the stars, we do not lose sight of our inner compass, guided by faith and a profound respect for creation.

Moving forward, the church has the opportunity to foster a new generation of faithful scientists and explorers who will carry the torch into the unknown. Educational initiatives and support for scientific endeavors, grounded in Catholic teachings, can nurture a seamless integration of faith and exploration.

Ultimately, the pioneers of faith in the space era remind us that our journey through space, like our spiritual journey, is one of discovery, awe, and an ever-deeper understanding of our place in the universe. They stand as testament to the belief that in the vast, magnificent expanse of space, there is still room for God, for faith, and for the spiritual growth of humanity.

As we gaze upwards at the night sky, let us remember those who have bravely ventured into this final frontier, not just with scientific instruments, but also with faith as their guide. Their legacy challenges us to contemplate our own place in the cosmos and to pursue our explorations with a sense of purpose and reverence that honors the Creator of all.

In the infinite breadth of space, we are invited to explore not only the physical universe but also the depths of our faith and our relationship with the Divine. The pioneers of faith in the space era serve as beacons of light, guiding us through this dual journey of outer and inner discovery.

Humanity's Place Among the Stars

In this age of exponential technological advancement, humanity stands on the precipice of a new era in the exploration of space, a domain that not only showcases the physical grandeur of creation but also represents the boundless providence of God the Creator. Within this context, the venture into the cosmos is not merely a pursuit of human curiosity but a profound invitation to expand our horizons and understand our place within the vastness of the universe. This invitation, deeply rooted in the tradition of Catholic teaching, challenges us to contemplate our role and responsibilities as stewards of creation, beyond the confines of our earthly home.

The call to explore the cosmos is interwoven with a fundamental respect for the creation that God has entrusted to humanity. As we look towards the stars, we are reminded of the Psalmist's awe-struck question: "What is man that you are mindful of him, and the son of man that you care for him?" (Psalm 8:4). This biblical reflection underscores the humility with which we should approach the universe, recognizing our smallness in the face of its vastness, yet also acknowledging the unique role that humans play in God's creative plan.

The endeavor of space exploration mirrors the intrinsic human desire to seek out the unknown, a longing placed in our hearts by the Creator Himself. This quest for knowledge and understanding is a testament to the image of God reflected in human intellect and creativity. However, this quest does not exist in isolation from our broader obligations to creation and to each other. As we reach for the stars, we must carry with us a profound commitment to respecting the integrity of the cosmos as part of God's creation.

Providence, as understood within the Catholic tradition, speaks to the sovereign and loving governance of God over creation. It is through this lens of Providence that we can view space exploration as part of the unfolding of God's plan for humanity and the universe. Each discovery made beyond the Earth's atmosphere is not just a scientific achievement but also a revelation of the beauty and complexity of God's creation, calling us to a deeper appreciation and reverence for the natural order.

The Catholic Church, throughout history, has maintained a dialogue with the sciences, recognizing the value of scientific discovery in deepening our understanding of God's creative work. The exploration of space presents a new frontier in this dialogue, offering unique opportunities to reflect on fundamental questions about creation, human nature, and the ultimate purpose of the universe. This reflection is an essential part of discerning our place among the stars, amidst the vast canvass of the cosmos that God has laid before us.

As humans venture further into space, the concept of stewardship takes on new dimensions. The care for our common home, as outlined in Laudato Si', extends beyond the Earth to include the entire cosmos, challenging us to develop an ethic of responsibility and care for the cosmic environment. This stewardship is a concrete expression of our partnership with God in the ongoing act of creation, ensuring that as we utilize the resources of the cosmos, we do so with respect and reverence for the Creator's design.

Moreover, the call to explore space is deeply aligned with the Church's mission to evangelize and witness to the love of God throughout creation. Just as missionaries of the past ventured into unknown lands to spread the Gospel, today's explorers carry with them the light of Christ to the furthest reaches of the universe. This mission is a powerful reminder that the message of salvation and the reality of God's love are not confined by terrestrial boundaries but extend infinitely throughout creation.

In contemplating humanity's place among the stars, it is essential to recognize that our journey into space is not merely a testament to human achievement but a pilgrimage of discovery, guided by the providential hand of God. Each step taken beyond our Earthly confines offers a unique opportunity to encounter the divine, to marvel at the complexity and beauty of God's creation, and to deepen our understanding of our role within this grand cosmic narrative.

Therefore, as we forge ahead, navigating the uncharted territories of space, we must do so with a spirit of humility and awe, recognizing that our quest for knowledge and exploration is ultimately a journey towards understanding our Creator better. Our place among the stars, while seemingly small in the vast expanse of the universe, is profoundly significant in the eyes of God, who has called us to explore, understand, and steward His creation with wisdom and reverence.

As humanity embarks on this grand venture, it is crucial to maintain a perspective that balances scientific inquiry with spiritual and ethical considerations. The challenge of becoming a multiplanetary species is not just a technological or scientific endeavor but also a deeply moral and spiritual one. It calls for a collective commitment to ensure that as we reach out into the cosmos, we do so with an eye towards the common good, guided by the principles of Catholic teaching and the light of faith.

In conclusion, humanity's place among the stars is far more than a physical location within the cosmic expanse; it is a profound statement about our purpose and destiny within God's creation. Through the grace of Providence, as we explore the heavens, we embark on a sacred journey to understand our place in the universe, which God has so marvelously designed. It is a journey that calls us to wisdom, stewardship, and awe—a true pilgrimage into the heart of creation.

The Call to Expand Horizons

In the intricate tapestry of creation, the boundless cosmos beckons humanity to explore, inviting us to expand our horizons beyond the familiar confines of Earth. This celestial invitation not only captivates the imagination but also speaks profoundly to the human spirit's inherent desire to seek out the unknown. The grandeur of the universe, as revealed through the lens of modern science, aligns harmoniously with the Catholic understanding of creation as an expression of Divine Providence. It is through this exploration that we come to understand our place among the stars, and how this pursuit aligns with God's will for us.

The inherent curiosity that leads us to explore the cosmos is not a mere coincidence but a directive woven into our very being by the Creator Himself. As stewards of creation, we are called to not only tend to the Earth but also to venture into the heavens. This journey holds the promise of unveiling the complexities of the universe, revealing further signs of God's infinite wisdom and power. In embracing the cosmos, we embark on a sacred endeavor, seeking to understand the works of the Almighty and our role within this vast creation.

Space exploration, in essence, extends the horizons of human knowledge and experience. It challenges us to reconsider our understanding of creation, life, and our place in the universe. Each discovery made beyond the confines of our planet serves as a testament to the boundless creativity of God, inviting us to ponder the full scope of Providence. In this pursuit, scientists and theologians alike are partners in unraveling the mysteries of creation, each contributing unique insights into the nature of the divine.

Yet, as we stand at the threshold of the cosmos, we are reminded of our responsibilities. The call to expand horizons is accompanied by an ethical imperative to respect creation in all its forms. The advent of space exploration brings to the fore questions of stewardship and moral conduct. How we explore and potentially inhabit other worlds speaks volumes about our respect for the Creator's work. We are tasked with exploring the heavens not as conquerors, but as humble seekers of knowledge, always mindful of the intrinsic value of all creation.

In this grand endeavor, Providence guides us. The belief in divine guidance reassures us of God's presence in every step of our cosmic journey. It is a journey not merely for acquiring scientific knowledge but for deepening our spiritual understanding as well. Through the exploration of the heavens, we are drawn closer to God, becoming more aware of the interconnectedness of all creation, and our unique role within it.

The expansion of humanity's horizons beyond Earth also reflects our collective hope and aspiration for the future. It is a tangible manifestation of our faith in possibilities, guided by the light of God's wisdom. As we venture into space, we carry with us the values and teachings of the Gospel, seeking to apply them in new contexts and environments. This journey offers an unparalleled opportunity for dialogue between faith and science, each enriching the other and providing a fuller understanding of our place in the cosmos.

Furthermore, the call to explore space resonates with the Biblical command to "fill the earth and subdue it" (Genesis 1:28). However, this command must be interpreted in the context of stewardship and respect for creation. As we seek to expand our physical horizons, we must also broaden our ethical horizons, ensuring that our actions in space reflect our commitment to nurturing and safeguarding all of God's creation.

The exploration of space also serves as a powerful reminder of our shared humanity. As we gaze upon Earth from the vantage point of space, national boundaries blur, and the planet appears as a single, fragile oasis in the vastness of space. This perspective fosters a sense of global solidarity and a realization of the need for cooperation in stewarding the Earth and exploring the heavens. It is a vivid illustration of the Catholic principle of the common good, underscoring the importance of working together for the benefit of all creation.

In conclusion, the call to expand horizons is a divine invitation to explore, understand, and ultimately cherish the universe as an integral part of God's creation. This endeavor, grounded in faith and guided by ethical principles, offers profound opportunities for spiritual growth and a deeper appreciation of the omnipresent hand of Providence. As humanity steps into the cosmos, we walk with God, embracing the mysteries of the universe and our place within it.

Our journey into space is not an escape from our responsibilities on Earth but a continuation of our vocation as stewards of creation. As we look to the stars, let us do so with reverence, humility, and a deep sense of purpose, ever mindful of our calling to care for all that God has made. The expansion of humanity's horizons is both a scientific endeavor and a spiritual pilgrimage—a quest not only for knowledge but for wisdom and a deeper communion with the Creator.

The cosmos, vast and mysterious, invites us to embark on this journey of discovery, guided by faith, reason, and a profound respect for the divine order. In advancing into new frontiers, let us hold fast to the eternal truths that ground us, allowing our exploration of the heavens to illuminate our path toward God.

For in seeking the stars, we are ultimately seeking the One who made them, finding in the immensity of the universe a reflection of God's infinite love and majesty.

Respecting Creation While Embracing the Cosmos As humanity's gaze extends beyond the confines of our earthly home, venturing into the vast expanses of space, it's imperative that our moral compass and ethical considerations evolve alongside our technological advancements. In the journey towards becoming a multiplanetary species, the Catholic tradition provides a framework that not only encourages exploration but also emphasizes the stewardship of creation.

In the Catholic understanding, the cosmos is not merely a void waiting to be filled by human ambition, but a creation imbued with God's presence and providence. As such, exploring the cosmos requires an attitude of humility and respect towards the masterpiece that is creation. This perspective demands recognition of the intricate balance and the inherent value of the universe, which goes beyond its potential utility to humans.

The exploration of space, while pushing the boundaries of human knowledge and presence, often brings with it the temptation to dominate and exploit. Yet, Catholic teaching offers a counter-narrative, one that views humanity as caretakers of creation rather than its conquerors. This stewardship ethic insists that in our quest to inhabit other worlds, we must ensure that our actions do not mar the sanctity of those celestial bodies or disrupt their ecosystems, should they exist.

Indeed, the concept of Providence plays a crucial role in how we approach the cosmos. It is believed that all creation is under the watchful eye of God, who guides and sustains the universe in a manner that human understanding can scarcely comprehend. This divine oversight suggests that our exploratory efforts must align with the Creator's will, advancing in a way that upholds the dignity of creation and serves the common good.

As humanity stands on the cusp of becoming a species not bound to a single planet, questions of ethical boundaries and responsibilities become increasingly pertinent. How do we apply the Catholic principle of the common good in the vast, seemingly empty expanse of space? This principle implies that the benefits of space exploration, and potentially colonization, should not be reserved for a privileged few but should enhance the wellbeing of all humanity. It challenges us to consider how advancements in space technology can address earthly inequalities and contribute to the flourishing of all peoples.

The moral imperative to honor and preserve the integrity of creation also extends to any extraterrestrial life we might encounter. The possibility of discovering life beyond Earth invites us to broaden our ethical considerations, recognizing the potential sanctity of alien life forms and their habitats. This speculative scenario challenges us to consider our actions carefully, ensuring that our explorations are conducted with respect and non-interference in mind. It reminds us that in the cosmic playground, humanity is not the arbiter of value but rather a participant in the grand tapestry of creation.

The dialogue between the Catholic faith and modern cosmology provides a rich foundation for addressing these challenges. It offers a lens through which we can examine our motivations, actions, and aspirations in the cosmos, ensuring they are grounded in respect for creation and aligned with the pursuit of the common good. This engagement between faith and science enriches our understanding of the universe and our place within it, prompting us to approach the cosmos not just as explorers, but as humble stewards of a vast, divinely ordered creation.

Moreover, the discipline of space exploration offers a unique opportunity for practicing what Pope Francis refers to as an "integral ecology." This approach emphasizes the interconnectedness of all aspects of creation, both earthly and celestial. Viewing our endeavors in space through this lens compels us to consider the environmental impacts of space exploration and to pursue practices that minimize harm to celestial bodies and the broader cosmos.

This integral ecology also informs our understanding of how actions in space reflect upon our care for our common home, Earth. It raises questions about the allocation of resources, both intellectual and material, towards space exploration in light of pressing environmental concerns at home. This is not to argue that one endeavor excludes the other but to promote a balanced approach that sees the exploration of space as a means to enhance our understanding and care for Earth.

Ultimately, respecting creation while embracing the cosmos calls for a paradigm of exploration infused with awe, responsibility, and ethical discernment. It invites a dialogue between faith and reason, where scientific achievements are celebrated not as feats of human triumph but as milestones in humanity's ongoing journey to understand and respect the divine order of creation. It underscores the belief that in the vast, mysterious expanse of the universe, there lies not just the potential for human habitation and exploration but the profound invitation to see the hand of the Creator in the wonders of the cosmos.

In summary, as we stand at the threshold of a new era in human history, the challenge before us is not only technological but profoundly spiritual and moral. Embracing the cosmos as a multiplanetary species necessitates a reevaluation of our role within creation, guided by the principles of Catholic teaching and the overarching providence of God. It is a journey not just across the physical vastness of space but into the depths of our ethical and spiritual convictions, challenging us to extend the respect and stewardship we owe to Earth to the entire cosmos.

In this cosmic quest, our actions and intentions must reflect a harmonious blend of ambition and humility, innovation and reverence, exploring new worlds while safeguarding the sanctity of all creation. This delicate balance is the cornerstone of respecting creation while embracing the cosmos, ensuring that as humanity reaches for the stars, we do so with a sense of responsibility and grace, mindful of our place in the grand cosmic design orchestrated by the Creator.

Chapter 6: Space Exploration and the Common Good

The journey into space, once a far-fetched dream, has become a mosaic of human achievement and aspirations. The pursuit of knowledge and exploration beyond our planet raises profound questions about our place in the universe and our responsibilities toward it. It invites us to ponder how our celestial endeavors reflect not just our ambitions but our commitment to the common good as envisioned through the lens of faith and reason.

In the grand scheme of creation, humanity's venture into space serves a dual purpose. It is a quest for understanding, driven by an innate curiosity about the universe and our place within it. It also holds the promise of benefiting humanity through advances in technology, opportunities for global cooperation, and the potential for discovering resources that could address earthly challenges. This pursuit, however, must be guided by a moral compass that ensures the dignity of human life and the integrity of creation are upheld.

The concept of the common good, deeply rooted in Catholic social teaching, provides a framework for evaluating the motives and outcomes of space exploration. It prompts us to ask: Who benefits from these endeavors, and at what cost? The exploration of space must not be an extension of earthly inequalities, nor should it exploit the cosmos devoid of respect for creation as a manifestation of Divine will.

Understanding the universe as God's creation positions humanity as stewards of a cosmic environment not our own, an insight that should inform our interactions with the heavens. This stewardship implies a responsibility to protect the integrity of space as a shared inheritance, avoiding its degradation or exploitation for the benefit of a privileged few.

Advancements in space technology and exploration offer immense potential for the common good, from improving Earth-based technologies to the possibility of safeguarding humanity's future. However, the pursuit of these advancements must be balanced with ethical considerations. The danger of space becoming a new frontier for exploitation and competition, rather than cooperation and mutual benefit, is real and must be intentionally addressed.

The Catholic tradition, with its emphasis on the unity and dignity of all creation, offers valuable insights into how we might navigate the ethical complexities of space exploration. It calls us to see space as a domain of wonder and exploration that ultimately belongs to God. This perspective encourages a cooperative approach to space exploration, one that transcends national rivalries and seeks the wellbeing of all humanity.

Moreover, the potential of space for scientific research and resources must be weighed against the responsibilities we hold to future generations. Just as the Earth's climate and resources demand our care and consideration for those who will come after us, so too do the environments we may encounter beyond our planet.

The exploration of space also presents a unique opportunity for global solidarity. Joint ventures in space exploration, such as the International Space Station, demonstrate how collaboration across cultures and nations can achieve incredible feats. These collaborations are a testament to what humanity can accomplish when united by a common goal that serves the broader good.

However, the enthusiasm for space exploration must be tempered with humility. The vastness of the universe, illuminated by our growing but still incomplete understanding, serves as a reminder of the limitations of human knowledge and power. The dominion God has granted humanity over creation is not one of reckless exploitation, but of caretaking and stewardship, a principle as applicable to the cosmos as it is to our home on Earth.

As we look to the stars, we are reminded of the Psalmist's reflection on humanity's place in creation: "What is man that you are mindful of him, and the son of man that you care for him?" (Psalm 8:4). This awe and humility, informed by faith, can guide our exploration of space in a manner that honors God and serves the common good.

The Catholic understanding of the universe as a coherent and purposeful creation leads to the conclusion that space, like Earth, is imbued with meaning and directed towards an end. The quest for knowledge and exploration, therefore, is not merely for humanity's sake but is part of a larger narrative of understanding God's creation and our place within it.

Space exploration, in light of Catholic teaching, is more than the pursuit of technological prowess or economic gain. It's a journey of discovery that asks deeper questions about creation, the nature of God, and humanity's collective vocation. It challenges us to approach space not as conquerors, but as humble pilgrims, seeking to understand the marvels of God's universe and to use that understanding for the genuine good of all humanity.

In conclusion, as humanity presses further into the universe, it carries with it a profound responsibility. The Catholic perspective, with its emphasis on the common good, stewardship, and the sanctity of creation, offers guiding principles for this journey. By anchoring our exploration of space in these values, we can ensure that our steps among the stars are taken with wisdom, foresight, and a commitment to the good of all creation.

Considering the lessons from the past and the ethical compass provided by faith, humanity's journey into space can be a reflection of our highest aspirations and values. It's a testament to what can be achieved when we look beyond ourselves and consider the welfare of the entire human family and the integrity of creation as we reach for the heavens.

Pursuing Knowledge for Humanity's Benefit

In the grand tapestry of creation, space exploration stands as a monumental testament to humanity's quest for knowledge and understanding. This endeavor, deeply entwined with both the scientific and the spiritual, demonstrates a profound commitment to uncovering the mysteries of the cosmos not merely for curiosity's sake, but for the betterment of all human society. The drive to explore space, to understand its vastness and complexity, reflects an intrinsic aspect of what it means to be human: the relentless pursuit of truth.

As we reach beyond our terrestrial borders, we embark on a journey that mirrors the infinite complexity and order of the universe itself—a universe created and sustained by the divine providence of God. This exploration, therefore, is not an act of hubris, but a humble acknowledgment of our role within creation and an earnest attempt to comprehend the works of the Creator for humanity's benefit (Scheid, 2016). It is through this endeavor that we can appreciate the grandeur of the cosmos, recognizing it as a sign of God's infinite wisdom and love for mankind.

Space exploration, in its essence, serves the common good by expanding our understanding of the universe, revealing not only the potential for new resources and habitats but also deepening our insight into the physical laws that govern existence. Each discovery propels us forward, offering revolutionary advancements in technology, medicine, and environmental science, thus reflecting the divine mandate to nurture and preserve the gift of creation (Scheid, 2016).

However, the pursuit of knowledge for humanity's benefit does not come without its ethical imperatives. It demands a careful consideration of our responsibilities toward all creation. As stewards of the universe, it is imperative that we approach space exploration with respect, caution, and an unwavering commitment to peace and sustainability. This stewardship is not just a moral duty but a reflection of our understanding of creation as an interconnected whole, guided by the hand of Providence (Scheid, 2016).

Viewing space exploration through the lens of Catholic teaching compels us to confront the challenges of exploring the heavens with wisdom and discernment. It is not enough to venture into the cosmos driven by mere ambition; our actions must be informed by a deep respect for the natural order and a dedication to advancing the common good. In doing so, we honor the Creator by valuing the inherent dignity and worth of all parts of creation, recognizing the universe itself as a sacred trust bestowed upon humanity.

The integration of faith and reason is crucial as we navigate the complexities of space exploration. This synthesis offers a balanced perspective that honors both the empirical evidence presented by science and the spiritual truths affirmed by faith. It propels us toward a future where the fruits of our explorations in space are shared equitably, ensuring that the advancements and resources derived from these endeavors are utilized in ways that uplift all of humanity, particularly the most vulnerable among us.

In pursuing knowledge for humanity's benefit, we also cultivate a deeper spiritual awareness. The awe and wonder inspired by the vastness of space can lead to profound moments of reflection, where the pursuit of scientific knowledge becomes entwined with the search for meaning and purpose. This spiritual dimension of space exploration beckons us to ponder our place in the universe, inviting us into a deeper relationship with the divine, who is both the origin and the ultimate end of all creation.

This journey, however, is not devoid of challenges. The potential for exploitation and the commodification of space and its resources pose significant ethical concerns. As we advance into the cosmos, it is crucial that our endeavors are guided by principles of justice and equity, ensuring that the benefits of space exploration are accessible to all, not monopolized by the privileged few. This commitment to justice is not only a moral imperative but also a reflection of God's desire for harmony and peace among all His creation.

The dialogue between the Church and the scientific community plays a pivotal role in shaping the future of space exploration. This collaboration enriches our understanding of the cosmos, fostering a culture of mutual respect and shared purpose. By bridging the perceived gap between faith and science, we can navigate the moral and ethical complexities of space exploration more effectively, ensuring that our advancements in this field are aligned with the greater good.

As we contemplate our cosmic journey, it is crucial to remember that space exploration is not merely a testament to human ingenuity and perseverance but also a profound expression of our collective aspiration for transcendence. It is a pursuit that calls us to look beyond ourselves, to reach out into the unknown with courage and hope, guided by the light of faith and the wisdom of reason. This quest, while marked by uncertainties, holds the promise of new horizons and the potential for incredible discoveries that can enrich the human experience in ways we have yet to imagine.

The providential view of the universe emphasizes that all creation is interconnected and directed towards a divine purpose. In this light, space exploration can be seen as a cooperative endeavor with God's creative work, a journey that is not only about expanding our physical boundaries but also about deepening our spiritual understanding and appreciation of creation. Through this pursuit, we fulfill part of our vocation to be co-creators, participating in the unfolding of the cosmic plan and contributing to the revelation of the divine mysteries.

In conclusion, pursuing knowledge for humanity's benefit through space exploration is a noble endeavor that reflects our deepest aspirations and values. It serves as a bridge between the temporal and the eternal, the material and the spiritual, inviting us to explore not only the outer reaches of the cosmos but also the inner depths of the human soul. As we venture forth into this vast, uncharted territory, let us do so with humility, gratitude, and a steadfast commitment to the common good, ever mindful of our responsibility as stewards of God's creation and ambassadors of hope for future generations.

The Dangers of Exploitation in Space As humanity extends its reach beyond Earth, venturing into the vast expanses of space, the thirst for knowledge and discovery must be tempered with caution and responsibility. The cosmos, in its infinite complexity and grandeur, bears witness to the creative power of God, inviting us to marvel and participate in its exploration. Yet, as we embark on this remarkable journey, we must remain vigilant against the dangers of exploitation that loom in the absence of ethical restraint.

The allure of space, with its untapped resources and uncharted territories, can easily breed a mentality of conquest rather than stewardship. The intrinsic value of celestial bodies, as part of God's creation, risks being overshadowed by their potential utility. This potential for exploitation carries with it significant moral implications, challenging us to reflect on our responsibilities not only to Earth but to the entire universe.

Historically, human endeavors in unknown frontiers have often been marked by exploitation and disregard for intrinsic values. The pursuit of space exploration, while driven by noble aspirations, is not immune to these pitfalls. It raises ethical questions about the appropriation of extraterrestrial resources, the commercialization of space, and the environmental impacts of space activities. As stewards of creation, it is incumbent upon us to approach these issues with a sense of duty and reverence for the cosmic order established by God.

The concept of the common good, deeply embedded in Catholic social teaching, provides a valuable framework for considering the implications of space exploration. Just as we are called to promote the common good on Earth, so too must we extend this principle to our endeavors in space. This involves recognizing the inherent dignity and worth of all creation and ensuring that our actions contribute to the flourishing of the universe as a whole.

In light of these considerations, the exploitation of space poses a challenge to the Catholic understanding of stewardship and the common good. It compels us to ask: How can we harness the benefits of space exploration in a way that respects the integrity of the cosmos? What measures can be implemented to prevent the commodification of space and the squandering of its resources?

One potential safeguard against exploitation is the development of a comprehensive ethical framework for space exploration. Such a framework would need to be grounded in the principles of Catholic social teaching, emphasizing respect for creation, the promotion of the common good, and the responsible use of resources. It would also require international cooperation and agreement, reflecting a collective commitment to the ethical stewardship of space.

Moreover, the notion of Providence has significant implications for our approach to space exploration. Recognizing that the universe is under God's care and guidance encourages a posture of humility and trust in the face of the unknown. It reminds us that, while we are co-creators with God, tasked with exploring and understanding the cosmos, our endeavors must always align with the divine will and purpose.

Another critical aspect of addressing the dangers of exploitation in space is the cultivation of an attitude of wonder and reverence for creation. The vastness of the universe, with its stars, planets, and galaxies, speaks of the majesty of God and the marvels of His work. Approaching space exploration with this sense of wonder can help to counteract the utilitarian mindset that sees only resources to be extracted and territories to be conquered.

Furthermore, the Catholic tradition of contemplation offers valuable insights for space explorers and those responsible for shaping space policy. Contemplation teaches us to see beyond the surface, recognizing the deeper meanings and connections that bind all creation. This spiritual perspective can inspire a more ethical and reverential approach to exploring the cosmos, one that sees space not as a frontier to be exploited but as a sacred realm to be cherished.

In conclusion, the dangers of exploitation in space compel us to confront complex ethical dilemmas and remind us of our responsibilities as stewards of creation. By grounding our efforts in the principles of Catholic social teaching, drawing on the notion of Providence, and fostering an attitude of wonder and reverence, we can navigate the challenges of space exploration in a way that honors God's creation and promotes the common good. As we venture further into the cosmos, let us carry forward the light of ethical discernment, guided by faith and a profound respect for the universe as a divine gift.

The Saints and the Stars: Spiritual Guidance on Our Cosmic Journey

In the silent language of the stars, there echoes a message of divine providence and the infinite complexity of creation. The journey into space, a dream nurtured within the heart of humanity, has always been more than a quest for knowledge - it is a pilgrimage into the vast cathedral of the universe. Guided by the teachings of the saints, our celestial voyage becomes a spiritual odyssey, a testament to the majesty of the Creator who orchestrates the harmony of the heavens.

The beauty and order that govern the cosmos have long fascinated both the scientist and the theologian. The saints, in their contemplative understanding of creation, have offered profound insights that illumine the path of modern cosmologists. As explorers of the physical universe, we must recognize that our quest for knowledge is ultimately a search for the Creator. The vast expanse of the cosmos, teeming with galaxies, stars, and planets, is a grand invitation to acknowledge the omnipotence of God.

The lives of the saints teach us that to embark on this cosmic journey, we must cultivate the virtues of humility and awe. In the depths of space, where the grand scale of creation dwarfs human ambition, these virtues anchor us to the truth of our existence - that we are part of a larger, divine tapestry. Each discovery in the realms beyond our Earth is a revelation that invites us into a deeper relationship with God.

The contemplation of the stars has always stirred within the human heart a sense of wonder and a desire to reach beyond what is seen. It is in this aspiration that we discover the congruence between scientific exploration and spiritual yearning. The saints and mystics, who reached out in love and longing for the divine, guide us in understanding that our endeavors in space are ultimately expressions of our intrinsic orientation towards the infinite.

The pursuit of knowledge, when guided by the virtues exemplified by the saints, transforms our journey into space into an act of worship. It is in the meticulous study of the stars and planets that we articulate our praise for the Creator. Every scientific endeavor, when undertaken with a spirit of humility and reverence, becomes a part of the cosmic liturgy, celebrating the creativity and wisdom of God.

As we venture further into the unknown, the saints encourage us to see God's handiwork in the precision of orbital mechanics, the beauty of a supernova, and the potential for life in distant worlds. Our exploration of space becomes an opportunity to encounter the Divine, to reflect on the Creator's generosity in sharing the wonders of the universe with us.

Yet, our journey is not without its ethical dimensions. The teachings of the saints remind us of our responsibility to steward creation. Just as we are called to care for our planet, we are entrusted with the preservation of the cosmos. The pursuit of knowledge must be balanced with the commitment to protect and honor the integrity of creation.

In the silence of space, we are invited to listen - to perceive the whisper of God in the harmony of the spheres. The saints teach us that in the quiet of contemplation, the truth of the universe reveals itself. Our hearts, attuned to the divine, understand that the laws governing the heavens are expressions of God's love and wisdom.

Our exploration of space is, therefore, a journey into the heart of the Church. It is within this spiritual embrace that we find the courage to embark on missions beyond our world. The saints, our heavenly companions, guide us, reminding us that in every endeavor, divine providence is our map and compass.

As we stand on the cusp of becoming a multiplanetary species, the insights of the saints into the nature of creation offer light to navigate the ethical challenges of this new horizon. They model for us a way of being that integrates our spiritual heritage with our aspirations among the stars.

The dialogue between faith and science enriches our understanding of the universe. It is through this confluence of perspectives that we approach the mystery of creation with a sense of humility and awe. The saints, with their deep love for God and His creation, reveal to us that the pursuit of scientific knowledge and the quest for spiritual truth are not disparate paths, but a unified journey towards understanding.

As we venture further into the cosmos, let us carry with us the wisdom of the saints - a wisdom that informs our science with ethics and imbues our exploration with a sense of purpose. Their lives remind us that our greatest discoveries are not merely out there among the stars, but also within the depths of the human heart, where the divine spark resides.

Ultimately, our cosmic journey is a pilgrimage, a sacred venture into the unknown, guided by the light of faith and the brilliance of the heavens. The saints and the stars beckon us onward, toward the heart of the divine mystery that is both the origin and the destiny of all creation.

Let us then embark on this journey with hearts open to the wonders that await and souls attuned to the spiritual guidance of the saints. In the vastness of space, we find a profound connection to the Creator, a reminder of our sacred duty to honor and cherish the gift of creation. It is a journey that beckons us ever upward, into the embrace of the infinite.

Lessons from Saints for Modern Cosmologists

In the endeavor to understand the cosmos, modern cosmologists stand on the shoulders of not only giants in their field but also those of profound spiritual insight. The saints, with their deep connection to the divine and contemplative view on creation, offer valuable perspectives that can enrich our understanding of the universe and our place within it. Their lives and teachings provide a unique lens through which we can examine the profound questions of existence that cosmology seeks to answer.

One of the cardinal lessons that saints impart to cosmologists is the virtue of humility. In the vastness of the cosmos, it's easy for scientists to either feel insignificant or, conversely, become enthralled by the power of human reason and technology. Saints like Thérèse of Lisieux taught the "little way", a path of recognizing one's limitations and the importance of simplest acts done with love. For cosmologists, this can translate to a scientific practice that acknowledges the vast unknown, the limitations of human knowledge and the ethical implications of their work.

The practice of contemplation, deeply rooted in the lives of many saints, is another treasure for the modern cosmologist. Contemplation involves a profound engagement with the subject of one's focus, seeing beyond the surface to the deeper truths. Saints like Ignatius of Loyola developed spiritual exercises that encouraged a contemplative gaze upon the world, recognizing the presence of the divine in all things. Cosmologists, too, can benefit from this contemplative approach, seeing beyond the mere mechanics of the cosmos to ponder the larger questions of why the universe exists and what it tells us about the nature of the divine.

Stewardship is a principle deeply embedded in the teachings of numerous saints and is especially pertinent to cosmologists exploring the fragility and vastness of our universe. Francis of Assisi, known for his special relationship with nature and all creatures, exemplifies a life of respect and care for creation. This stewardship, when applied to the realm of cosmology, underscores the responsibility of scientists to not only explore but also protect the cosmic environment and consider the long-term consequences of their explorations on the cosmic order.

The concept of unity and interconnectedness finds resonance in the teachings of saints and is crucial for cosmologists. Saints like Teresa of Ávila and John of the Cross spoke of the soul's deep connection to God and all creation, emphasizing a holistic view of the universe. Cosmologists exploring the fundamental forces of the universe can draw inspiration from this spiritual insight, recognizing that the laws governing the cosmos reflect a deep interconnectedness and harmony.

Another enlightening lesson comes from the embrace of mystery. Saints like Augustine of Hippo grappled with the mysteries of faith, recognizing that not all could be understood or explained. This acceptance of mystery is vital for cosmologists facing the enigmatic aspects of the universe, such as dark matter, dark energy, and the conditions of the big bang. It encourages a scientific practice open to mystery, one that views the unexplained not as a defeat but as an invitation to deeper understanding and humility.

Furthermore, the concept of universal call to holiness, as articulated by saints throughout ages, underscores the idea that every individual has a unique role in the grand design of creation, including those involved in the scientific exploration of the universe. This perspective invites cosmologists to see their work not just as a pursuit of knowledge, but as a vocation with intrinsic value and purpose, contributing to the larger cosmic and spiritual story.

The virtue of hope, exemplified by saints across centuries, is critically important for cosmologists facing the vast, often daunting, expanse of the universe. Saints like Maximilian Kolbe, who maintained hope amidst the darkness of a concentration camp, teach that even in the face of great unknowns and challenges, hope is a powerful force. For cosmologists, embedding hope in their quest for understanding can be a beacon guiding their explorations and the interpretation of their findings.

Lastly, saints' lives teach the importance of integrating faith and reason—a balance that is foundational for cosmologists navigating between empirical evidence and the larger philosophical and theological implications of their work. Saints like Thomas Aquinas, who articulated a sophisticated synthesis of faith and reason, remind us that the pursuit of scientific knowledge and the quest for spiritual understanding are not opposing endeavors but are complementary paths to truth.

In conclusion, the saints, with their rich spiritual heritage, offer cosmologists valuable lessons that can inspire and guide their exploration of the cosmos. By integrating humility, contemplation, stewardship, an understanding of interconnectedness, an embrace of mystery, a sense of vocation, hope, and a balance of faith and reason, modern cosmologists can navigate the vast reaches of space with a deepened sense of purpose and ethical responsibility. The dialogue between the spiritual wisdom of the saints and the empirical inquiry of cosmology enriches our collective understanding of the universe and our place within it, pointing us towards a holistic vision of creation that embraces both the wonders of the cosmos and the transcendent mystery of the divine.

Finding God in the Vastness of Space

In the journey through the cosmos, humanity carries within it the deep-seated quest not only for knowledge but also for meaning. The vastness of space, with its billions of galaxies, stars, and the ever-present awe of creation, challenges us to ponder our existence and the existence of a Creator. This awe-inspiring exploration into the unknown stretches our understanding of the world around us and the divine. It is here, in the vastness of space, that we find echoes of the divine majesty, a silent testament to the almighty creator of all things.

The act of gazing upon the stars has, throughout history, inspired a sense of wonder and divine presence. It's a humbling experience that places our fleeting existence into perspective against the backdrop of the cosmos. The exploration of space, thus, becomes not just a scientific endeavor but a spiritual pilgrimage in search of understanding, driven by the conviction that the universe's intricate design points towards a higher power.

Within the cold, seemingly indifferent expanses of space, the presence of God may not be immediately obvious to the empirical observer. Yet, faith teaches that the Creator permeates all creation, holding the universe in existence by the power of His will. This unity of creation, underlined by laws that govern celestial movements, reflects divine thought, an intentional act of creation that calls everything into being from nothingness.

It's in this understanding that we see the role of divine providence within the cosmos. Providence, the protective care of God, is not absent in the aeons of cosmic time. Each star born and each galaxy formed moves under the guidance of God's eternal laws, manifesting His wisdom and power. In the face of the overwhelming scale of the universe, the providential care of God assures us that no part of creation, no matter how miniscule, escapes His notice.

The exploration of space thus serves a dual purpose. Scientifically, it expands our knowledge of the universe, pushing the boundaries of what is known. Spiritually, it reaffirms our belief in a creator who is both immanent and transcendent, intimately involved with His creation while surpassing all understanding. This duality enhances the Catholic understanding of God's nature and His relationship with creation.

The scientific achievements in space exploration, from landing on the moon to the images captured by the Hubble Space Telescope, showcase humanity's incredible capability for discovery. These milestones do not diminish God's role in creation but rather illuminate the grandeur of His work, inviting deeper reflection on the Creator's power and wisdom.

This contemplation leads us to recognize the inherent value and dignity of the cosmos as part of God's creation. It challenges us to approach space not as a domain to be conquered or exploited, but as a sacred realm, a gift to be respected and treasured. The ethical imperatives of exploring the heavens become intertwined with our duty to stewardship, guided by an awareness of our place within the divine order.

In embracing the cosmic journey, we encounter the opportunity to expand the horizons of our faith. The magnificence of creation, from the smallest particle to the vast galaxies, speaks to the limitless imagination of God. It invites us to wonder, to seek, and ultimately, to come to a deeper understanding of our Creator.

Furthermore, the challenge of interpreting our observations and experiences in space through the lens of Catholic teaching enriches our theological understanding. It offers a unique vantage point from which to contemplate the mysteries of faith, encouraging dialogue between the realms of science and spirituality.

This dialogue is crucial in today's age, where scientific discovery and technological advancements are accelerating. It allows us to frame our endeavors in space within the context of our faith, ensuring that as we reach for the stars, we remain grounded in our spiritual convictions and responsibilities.

The pursuit of knowledge in the vastness of space, therefore, becomes an extension of our search for God. It is a journey that aligns with the deepest desires of the human heart: to know, to love, and to serve the Creator. As we explore the universe, we are drawn closer to the Divine, guided by the light of stars and the wisdom of our faith.

In conclusion, finding God in the vastness of space is a journey that transcends physical boundaries. It is an invitation to explore, to marvel, and to worship. As we stand on the threshold of new cosmic discoveries, we are reminded of the infinite power and presence of God in the universe, calling us to a deeper faith, a wider understanding, and a more profound awe of the Divine Majesty.

The cosmos, in its breathtaking beauty and complexity, becomes a cathedral of creation, a sacred space where science and faith converge. In this sanctuary, we are offered a glimpse of the eternal, an encounter with the Almighty, who invites us to look beyond ourselves and our world, to the very heart of existence, where God waits to be found.

In venturing into the vastness of space, we are not left adrift but are guided by the light of faith, which illuminates our path. This journey, steeped in wonder and worship, challenges us to view creation not as mere matter and void but as a testament to God's love and grandeur, an ever-expanding canvas of divine artistry on which our stories unfold — a cosmic pilgrimage towards understanding and unity with the Creator.

Providence and the Physical Universe

The contemplation of the cosmos, in its vastness and mystery, naturally evokes a profound sense of wonder and curiosity. It's an exploration not solely of the physical, but of the metaphysical, where the concept of providence interweaves with the fabric of the universe. The belief in a benevolent orchestration of the cosmos by a divine Creator stands at the heart of Catholic teaching, presenting a view of the universe that is not chaotic nor indifferent, but purposeful and guided by an all-knowing, all-powerful hand.

In the endeavor to understand the universe, the scientific method and the tenets of faith might seem, at first glance, to tread diverging paths. Yet, in the Catholic tradition, there's a harmonious dialogue that bridges these realms. Divine providence does not negate the laws of nature; instead, it encompasses and transcends them, affirming that the laws governing the physical universe are themselves expressions of a higher order and wisdom.

The principle of providence elucidates the belief that every event in the physical universe is under God's care and direction. From the gravitational forces that bind galaxies, to the atomic interactions that fuel stars, and down to the minute details of a sparrow's existence, nothing escapes His governance. This perspective encourages a reflection on the interconnectedness of all creation and the purpose behind cosmic and human history.

Space exploration and efforts to expand humanity into a multiplanetary species challenge us to reconsider our understanding of providence in the context of the vast, uncharted cosmic expanse. The pursuit of knowledge beyond our world, while a testament to human ingenuity, also humbles us before the immensity of creation and the intricacies of its design that we are only beginning to uncover.

Within this grand pursuit, the concept of providence raises pivotal questions about human agency and the limits of control over the cosmos. The recognition of divine providence fosters a profound respect for the natural universe, not merely as a domain to be conquered or exploited, but as a sacred creation imbued with meaning and purpose beyond our full comprehension.

This outlook shapes a Catholic approach to cosmic exploration, one that sees humanity as stewards rather than proprietors of the universe. It calls for a responsible engagement with space, wherein our actions are guided by ethical considerations that reflect an understanding of creation as ultimately deriving its value and significance from its Creator.

The narratives of space exploration, filled with achievements and aspirations, are thus seen not merely as human endeavors but as chapters in a larger cosmic story authored by Providence. This story, penned with the ink of physical laws and the parchment of galaxies, invites humanity to partake in the unfolding mystery of creation, with a sense of duty and reverence.

Yet, the concept of providence should not be misconstrued as a deterministic script that negates human freedom. Rather, it affirms the coexistence of free will within the parameters of divine foresight and care. Our explorations and discoveries, our trials and triumphs in space and on Earth, are elements of a dynamic relationship with the Creator, who invites us into a participatory role in creation's unfolding narrative.

The challenges faced in making humanity a multiplanetary species further illuminate the intricacies of providence in the cosmos. As we navigate the ethical and existential questions posed by establishing human presence on other worlds, we are prompted to reflect on the providential order that guides not only our home planet but the entire universe. This reflection deepens our understanding of our place within the cosmic scheme and the responsibilities that accompany such an extraordinary endeavor.

Embracing the cosmos through the lens of providence also encourages a reevaluation of our perspective on alien life forms and the sanctity of other worlds. If all creation is under the loving gaze and guidance of Providence, then our interactions with extraterrestrial environments and potential inhabitants must be approached with humility, respect, and a commitment to preserving the integrity of God's creation across the cosmos.

Ultimately, the exploration of space as informed by the Catholic conception of providence is not merely an outward journey across the stars but an inward journey of the soul towards a deeper kinship with the Creator. It's an opportunity to witness the divine artistry expressed in the vastness of the universe and to respond with awe, stewardship, and a commitment to the common good of all creation.

In this cosmic context, providence serves as a guiding light, revealing a universe imbued with order, purpose, and beauty. The scientific quest to understand the physical laws of the universe and the spiritual quest to discern the will of the Creator converge on the same path—a path that leads to a profound appreciation of the cosmos as a manifestation of divine wisdom and love.

As we navigate the future of space exploration, the lens of providence offers a framework that not only deepens our understanding of the universe but also enriches our spiritual life. It reminds us that our journey among the stars is ultimately a pilgrimage—a journey towards encountering the divine presence woven into the fabric of the cosmos, inviting us to partake in the grand adventure of creation.

This chapter, in drawing connections between providence and the physical universe, endeavors to illuminate the role of divine guidance in the cosmic order and humanity's place within it. It is a reflection on the boundless wisdom that orchestrates the cosmos, inviting us to marvel at creation, engage with it responsibly, and seek our ultimate purpose and destiny within the vast theatre of the universe.

Understanding Divine Providence in Creation

In the grand narrative of the cosmos, the intricate balance and order speak volumes of a meticulous design, a notion that has perennially engaged both the scientific mind and the spiritual heart. It's in the contemplation of this profound harmony that one can't help but reflect on the concept of Divine Providence. Providence, in its essence, represents God's sustaining and guiding presence throughout the fabric of creation, ensuring the fulfillment of His divine will. This perspective is not merely a theological abstraction but a principle that intertwines with the very laws governing the physical universe.

At the heart of understanding Divine Providence in creation is recognizing the omnipotence and omniscience of God. The belief that God created the universe out of nothing, ex nihilo, as a free act of love, sets the foundation for acknowledging His continued involvement in its unfolding. It isn't that the universe is a clock set in motion, left to run its course independently. Rather, it's seen as a living testament to God's ongoing engagement with creation, where every law, every particle, and every celestial body bears the imprint of Divine will.

This understanding implicitly refutes the notion of a distant deity, disengaged from the workings of the world. Instead, it paints a picture of a God who is intimately involved in the details of His creation, guiding it toward its ultimate purpose. The laws of physics, the constants of the universe, and the peculiar conditions that make life possible on Earth are perceived not as happy accidents but as markers of providential design.

The interplay between Divine Providence and the laws of nature poses intriguing questions for both theology and science. It suggests that the natural order, with its predictability and empirical scrutability, is itself a testament to Divine wisdom. This doesn't depreciate the value of scientific inquiry but enriches it with a deeper existential significance. Studying the universe becomes a way of unravelling the intricacies of God's creative expression, a pursuit that is both intellectually and spiritually rewarding.

As humans venture further into the cosmos, the concept of Providence also offers a framework for understanding our role within this vast creation. The endeavor to become a multiplanetary species, intertwined with advancements in space exploration, can be seen as part of a divine plan, urging humanity to reach beyond our terrestrial confines. This vision imbues our cosmic journey with a sense of purpose that transcends mere survival or curiosity. It's about participating in the unfolding of Divine Providence, exploring the universe as co-creators with God, and stewarding creation responsibly.

However, this expansive vision does not overshadow the minutiae of Divine Providence in individual lives. Just as God guides the universe, He is also present in the daily affairs of human existence, guiding, sustaining, and nurturing. This dual aspect of Providence, macrocosmic and microcosmic, reinforces a sense of meaning and interconnectedness in the universe.

Central to Catholic teaching is the belief that God's ultimate purpose for creation, and indeed for humanity, is communion with Himself. This eschatological view sees the physical universe not as an end in itself but as a pathway leading to an eternal destiny. The physical laws governing the cosmos, then, are not merely mechanical constraints but instruments of Divine love, guiding creation towards its fulfillment in God.

Understanding Divine Providence in creation also necessitates a discussion on free will. The capacity for humans to make choices and the presence of evil and suffering in the world raise difficult questions about God's providential plan. Yet, Catholic theology maintains that Divine Providence encompasses human freedom, weaving it into God's grand design without compromising it. This delicate balance underscores a profound truth: that human history, with all its complexity, is ultimately guided by God's loving will.

The exploration of the cosmos, thereby, becomes an act deeply infused with faith. It's a testament to human ingenuity and the longing to reach for the stars, yes, but also a profound act of faith in Divine Providence. Each discovery, each milestone in our cosmic journey, reflects the intricate dance between God's will and human freedom—a dance that guides the universe towards its fullness in God.

In this light, the ethical imperatives of exploring the heavens, respecting creation, and stewarding the universe responsibly are not merely practical concerns but spiritual obligations. They call for a recognition of our place within a providentially guided cosmos, tasked with a divine mandate to care for creation. This ethic, grounded in the recognition of Divine Providence, shapes a Catholic approach to the physical universe—one that marries faith with reason, spirituality with science.

As we look to the future, the principles of Divine Providence offer a hopeful perspective on the challenges and opportunities that lie in the cosmic expanse. Whether dealing with the ethical considerations of colonizing other worlds or grappling with the ecological impacts of space exploration, the guiding hand of Providence provides a compass. It assures us that, in the grand scheme of creation, nothing is arbitrary or without purpose. Every step taken in the vastness of space is part of a divine narrative, unfolding towards its ultimate realization in God.

In conclusion, understanding Divine Providence in creation offers a profound lens through which to view the universe. It challenges us to see beyond the mere physicality of the cosmos, to discern the guiding hand of God in the laws of nature, the trajectory of galaxies, and the quest of humanity to explore the heavens. It's a testament to the belief that the universe, in all its vastness and mystery, is a coherent, purpose-driven creation, moving inexorably towards its fulfillment in divine love.

The Limits of Human Control in the Cosmos

As mankind reaches out into the vast expanse of space, venturing far beyond the cradle of Earth, it's crucial to reckon with the intrinsic limits imposed upon us in the cosmos. This realization is not solely born from technological or scientific constraints but is also deeply rooted in theological, philosophical, and ethical considerations. Throughout history, humanity has constantly faced the humbling truth that, despite our advancements, there are forces and realms beyond our mastery. This truth is especially pertinent in the era of space exploration, where the allure of the unknown beckons us, and yet, the doctrine of Providence reminds us of our place within God's creation.

The endeavor to explore space and potentially become a multiplanetary species ignites the imagination and drives innovation. However, it equally raises profound questions about the limits of human control and dominion in the vast, unfathomable cosmos. From a Catholic perspective, we are taught that creation is an expression of God's infinite wisdom and power. The universe, in its grandeur and complexity, functions under divine Providence, an order established by God that guides and sustains all of creation (Catechism of the Catholic Church, 1992).

Scientific exploration, including the quest into outer space, is inherently a part of human nature. Our intelligence and curiosity, gifts from the Creator, compel us to explore, understand, and marvel at the universe around us. This pursuit of knowledge aligns with the Catholic understanding of participating in God's creation, uncovering the magnificence and order designed by the Almighty. However, as stewards of this creation, our endeavor to explore and possibly inhabit new worlds must be approached with humility, recognizing our subordination to Divine Providence.

Human efforts in the cosmos, whether it's sending probes to distant planets or planning human settlements on Mars, showcase our remarkable capabilities and potential. Yet, this vast universe, with its countless galaxies, stars, and planets, operates according to physical laws that are immutable and beyond our control. The cosmological constant, the speed of light, and the fundamental forces that govern the universe dictate what is possible within the cosmos. These are not merely scientific facts but also reminders of a greater order established by God, constraining what humanity can achieve.

Humanity's place in the universe, as informed by Catholic teachings, is one of both significance and humility. We are made in the image of God and given dominion over Earth (Genesis 1:26-28), yet this dominion does not extend unconditionally across the universe. Our authority and capabilities, while considerable on our home planet, meet their limits in the cosmic scale. It's a stark reminder that, despite our advancements and aspirations, we are part of a creation far grander and more intricate than our earthly domain.

The principle of Providence underscores that God is actively involved in the universe, guiding its history and development towards its ultimate fulfillment in Him. This belief does not negate human freedom or the validity of scientific exploration but places it within a context where human actions are part of a broader, divine narrative. As we explore space and encounter the limits of our capabilities and control, it becomes an opportunity for reflection on our dependency on God and the purpose He has entrusted to us.

Space exploration, in light of Catholic teaching, therefore, is not merely a technical or political endeavor but a deeply spiritual quest. It challenges us to expand our understanding of creation, our role within it, and how we might cooperate with divine Providence. While humans strive to push the boundaries of what is known and where we can go, we are constantly reminded of the ultimate sovereignty of God over all creation. This humbling realization does not diminish our quest but enriches it with purpose and perspective.

The Catholic perspective encourages a balance between the pursuit of knowledge and the acknowledgment of our inherent limitations within the cosmos. This balance is not a constraint but a liberation from the hubris that can accompany human achievements. As we reach out into the stars, we do so with a spirit of humility, stewardship, and a profound sense of our place in the universe, under the watchful eye of Providence.

Our attempts to make humanity a multiplanetary species must also consider the moral and ethical dimensions of such endeavors. It's an expression of our God-given curiosity and stewardship but also requires careful deliberation about the impact on potential extraterrestrial environments and their hypothetical inhabitants. Respecting creation beyond Earth is an extension of our responsibility as stewards of God's creation, a duty that does not end at the edge of our atmosphere.

The exploration of space invites a reflection on the transcendence and immanence of God. The vast expanses of the universe, with their awe-inspiring beauty and complexity, reveal a Creator who is both beyond all and intimately present in every aspect of creation. This paradoxical truth enriches the Catholic understanding of God and challenges us to find Him not only in the vastness of space but also in the minutiae of our exploration efforts and scientific discoveries.

In the pursuit of becoming a multiplanetary species, humanity is embarking on a journey that is as spiritual as it is physical. It's a journey that asks us to trust in the Providence of God while navigating the unknown. The limits we encounter along the way serve not as barriers but as beacons, guiding our path in humility and wisdom.

Ultimately, our explorations in the cosmos serve a greater purpose than mere survival or scientific curiosity. They are a testament to the human spirit, created in the image of God, striving to understand and participate in the divine order of creation. As we venture forth, we do so with faith that our steps are guided by Providence, leading us towards greater knowledge, reverence, and love for the Creator and all of creation.

In conclusion, the limits of human control in the cosmos, as understood through the lens of Catholic teaching, offer a profound opportunity for reflection and growth. They remind us of our place within a creation far grander than ourselves, guided by a Providence that extends beyond our understanding. As we continue to explore the stars, our journey is enriched by the knowledge that we are part of a greater cosmic order, ordained and sustained by God Himself.

Ethical Boundaries in Colonizing Other Worlds

The endeavor to colonize other worlds is not merely a scientific or technological quest but a deeply ethical and moral journey that encompasses the vast expanse of both human intellect and divine will. As humanity stands on the brink of becoming a multiplanetary species, it becomes imperative to explore the ethical boundaries that this monumental leap entails. This exploration must be guided by the light of the Gospel and the perennial Catholic teaching, which together articulate the sovereignty of God as the creator and final end of all creation.

In the context of colonizing other worlds, several ethical considerations come to the fore. First and foremost among these is the respect for alien worlds and their potential inhabitants. Just as the Catholic faith teaches respect for our common home on Earth and all its creatures, so too must this respect extend to other planets and their ecosystems. The concept of "space as a common home" suggests a shared responsibility among all of humanity to steward the cosmos with the same care and reverence we are commanded to show our earthly domain.

One cannot overlook the role of Providence in the unfolding narrative of human space exploration. Divine Providence, which governs the world with gentle order and purpose, must also inform our actions as we reach beyond Earth. This suggests that while humans possess the capability to explore and even colonize other planets, they must do so with a profound sense of humility and purpose, always seeking to align their endeavors with the will of God.

The ethical discourse surrounding the colonization of other worlds also raises questions about the rights of potential extraterrestrial life forms. If other sentient beings are encountered, Catholic teaching would insist on their inherent dignity and the universality of God's love extending to all of creation. This unprecedented situation would require a radical expansion of our ethical horizons, recognizing these beings as part of the cosmic family entrusted to our care by the Creator.

Furthermore, the concept of "terraforming" — the process of altering the environment of a planet to make it habitable for humans — poses significant ethical dilemmas. This process would necessitate a careful discernment of the rights of nature and the limits of human intervention in other worlds. Just as Earthly creation is not merely an object for exploitation but a gift to be cherished and protected, so too should the ecosystems of other planets be approached with a sense of stewardship and responsibility.

The potential for cultural imperialism is another critical ethical consideration. As societies extend their reach to other worlds, there lies a danger of imposing Earth-centric values and lifestyles on new planets. The colonization of other worlds must be approached with an ethic of respect and dialogue, rather than domination or coercion. This approach is echoed in the Catholic tradition of encountering and respecting diverse cultures, guided by principles of love and mutual respect.

Moreover, the distribution of resources and the benefits of space exploration pose significant ethical questions about justice and equity. The Catholic social teaching that emphasizes the common good and the preferential option for the poor should inform how resources from space exploration are utilized and shared. The bounty of the cosmos, like the gifts of Earth, are to be shared equitably, ensuring that the fruits of space exploration contribute to the flourishing of all humanity, not just the privileged few.

In conclusion, as humanity embarks on the quest to colonize other worlds, it must do so with a profound respect for the ethical implications of such endeavors. The Catholic tradition, with its rich teachings on creation, human dignity, and the common good, provides valuable guidance in navigating these uncharted ethical terrains. It is through adhering to these principles, under the watchful eye of Providence, that humanity can responsibly approach the colonization of new worlds, ensuring that this monumental achievement serves the greater glory of God and the universal common good.

Respecting Alien Worlds and Their Potential Inhabitants

In the grand narrative of human exploration, the leap into the cosmic ocean represents not just a step, but a giant leap for mankind. As we stand on the precipice of extending our reach to other worlds, it's paramount that we navigate these uncharted waters with a blend of scientific rigor, philosophical depth, and biblical wisdom. The task before us is not merely one of discovery but of profound ethical consideration.

The Catholic Church teaches us that all of creation is imbued with the divine signature of its Creator. It's a canvas that tells the story of God's grandeur, a narrative woven into every star, planet, and potentially, each form of life that dwells beyond our Earth. In this light, our interactions with alien worlds and their potential inhabitants are not just subjects of scientific interest but are deeply theological and moral in nature.

Space exploration, while a testament to human ingenuity and curiosity, carries with it a solemn responsibility. The potential discovery of life elsewhere in the universe raises profound questions about stewardship, respect, and the interconnectedness of all God's creations. As stewards of creation, humans are called to protect and respect the integrity of each world we encounter, recognizing them as part of the broader cosmic creation that God has entrusted to us.

This stewardship extends beyond mere non-interference; it encompasses a commitment to ensuring that our exploratory and potentially colonization efforts do not harm other worlds. The principle of "do no harm" transcends planetary boundaries and becomes a guiding ethos in our engagements with extraterrestrial environments and beings. This is rooted in the understanding that the value and sanctity of creation are not constrained by geography - whether terrestrial or extraterrestrial.

The possibility of encountering other intelligent beings in the cosmos poses additional ethical considerations. Such a discovery would challenge us to reconsider notions of personhood, community, and our place in the universe. Engaging with alien species in a manner that respects their autonomy and rights, assuming they are capable of possessing such concepts, is a non-negotiable moral imperative. This approach reflects the Gospel's teachings on love, respect, and the recognition of God's image in the other, no matter how alien that 'other' might seem.

Furthermore, the potential sacramental implications of non-human intelligent life challenge us to expand our understanding of salvation history. The Catholic faith, while terrestrial in its origin and early history, exists within the infinite context of God's creation. The inclusion of other worlds and their inhabitants in this salvific narrative necessitates an openness to the workings of Divine Providence beyond our planet.

Our pursuit of knowledge in the cosmos should be driven not by a desire for dominion or exploitation but by a quest for understanding, communion, and cooperation. The universe, in its immense diversity and complexity, reflects the boundless creativity of the Almighty. Respecting alien worlds and their potential inhabitants becomes a form of worship, a recognition of the Creator's handiwork in the vast tapestry of creation.

Protecting the integrity of alien worlds also aligns with the Church's teachings on the common good and environmental stewardship. Just as we are called to care for our Earthly home and all its inhabitants, so too are we responsible for ensuring that our actions do not jeopardize the ecological or social balances of other planets. This cosmic dimension of Catholic social teaching reminds us that our responsibilities as stewards extend to the farthest reaches of space.

Scientific exploration must, therefore, be accompanied by an ethical framework that prioritizes the protection of alien environments. This means implementing stringent protocols to prevent the contamination of extraterrestrial ecosystems by Earth-based lifeforms. Such precautions are akin to the principle of primum non nocere - first, do no harm - applied on a cosmic scale.

In dialogues about space exploration and colonization, the Catholic perspective offers a unique vantage point, one that harmonizes scientific inquiry with deep ethical and theological reflection. It insists on a dialogue between faith and reason, challenging both to expand their horizons in the recognition of and respect for the sacredness of all creation.

As we venture further into the cosmos, our actions must be informed by a profound reverence for the mystery and majesty of God's creation. This journey is not just a technical or scientific endeavor but a deeply spiritual one, calling us to reflect on our place in the universe, the nature of our relationship with the Creator, and our duties to all forms of life we might encounter.

In conclusion, respecting alien worlds and their potential inhabitants is not merely an option among many; it is a moral imperative that stems from our understanding of creation as a divine gift. It challenges us to be both humble and bold - humble in recognizing our smallness in the vast scope of the cosmos, and bold in taking up the stewardship entrusted to us by God. Thus, as we stand on the threshold of new worlds, let us move forward with awe, responsibility, and an unwavering commitment to respect the entirety of God's creation.

The Concept of "Space as a Common Home"

In the contemplation of the cosmos, humanity stands at the threshold of an era marked by both immense opportunity and profound responsibility. The expanses of space, once deemed unreachable and solely the domain of celestial beings, now beckon human exploration and habitation. This newfound realm, however, is not merely a frontier for technological conquest or a repository of resources to be exploited. Rather, it presents an imperative to recognize space as "a common home," a shared domain that calls for stewardship, ethical exploration, and an acknowledgment of its creator.

The principle of space as a common home draws deeply from the wellspring of Catholic social teaching, which emphasizes the common good, stewardship of God's creation, and the intrinsic value of every part of the cosmos. Just as the Earth is regarded as a shared home, requiring care and respect for its delicate balances and the life it supports, so too must the vastness of space be approached with a similar ethos. The ventures beyond our atmosphere, therefore, are not merely exercises in human curiosity or the pursuit of national prestige, but a collective moral enterprise.

In this pursuit, the concept of Divine Providence plays a pivotal role. Providence, in the Catholic understanding, refers to God's continual involvement with all created things, guiding them toward their ultimate perfection. This Providence does not negate human freedom or scientific endeavor but rather ensures that the cosmos and its exploration align with the purpose for which God created them. Recognizing space as a common home entails seeing it as part of God's providential plan, a vast canvas reflecting the glory and creativity of its maker and entrusted to humanity as stewards, not as conquerors.

The stewardship of space, much like that of Earth, demands a profound respect for creation. It involves a recognition of the intrinsic worth of the cosmos, beyond its utility to human ends. Just as the Earth's environment is a complex web of interdependence and balance, so too is the wider cosmos. Disrupting this balance not only disrespects the creation but also disrupts the Divine plan set forth by Providence. This understanding mandates a critical examination of how humans approach space exploration, ensuring that it is conducted responsibly, ethically, and in a manner that contributes to the common good.

Moreover, seeing space as a common home underscores the necessity for an inclusive dialogue regarding its exploration and use. This entails a collaborative international effort that transcends borders and acknowledges the shared heritage of the cosmos. Such an approach is in stark contrast to the divisive claims of ownership or unilateral exploitation of outer space resources. It embodies the Catholic principle of the universal destination of goods, extending it beyond Earth to encompass the cosmos. This universal perspective ensures that the benefits of space exploration are shared equitably, reflecting the inherent dignity of all humanity.

Furthermore, the notion of space as our common home enriches the Catholic understanding of creation's sanctity. It extends the duty of care and reverence for life from the biosphere of Earth to the life that might exist, or could one day exist, beyond it. This perspective invites a humility before the mystery of creation and a willingness to protect and preserve not just for the present but for future generations. It challenges human ingenuity to find ways of living in space that echo the Edenic call to till and keep, to serve and protect.

Central to this vision is the principle of subsidiarity, which emphasizes actions taken at the lowest level possible but also stresses the need for collective action when challenges are beyond the capacity of individuals or single nations. The environmental challenges faced on Earth, such as climate change, provide a somber lesson on the consequences of neglecting our common home. In space, this principle necessitates global cooperation in governance, ensuring that exploration and resource use are regulated to prevent a tragedy of the commons on a cosmic scale.

The Catholic vision of space as a common home also casts light on the moral dimensions of space tourism and colonization. These endeavors are not problematic in themselves but require a discernment of intentions and outcomes. They raise questions about equitable access, the potential for exacerbating inequalities, and the ethical implications of altering extraterrestrial environments. As humanity steps further into the cosmos, it must do so with a compassion that seeks the good of all, reflecting the inclusive love that the creator has for creation.

In conclusion, the conceptualization of space as a common home is not merely an ethical framework for the future of cosmic exploration but a profound spiritual reflection on humanity's place in the universe. It calls for a harmonious blend of scientific enthusiasm and moral wisdom, guided by Catholic teachings and the concept of Divine Providence. This perspective fosters a culture of respect, responsibility, and radical hope—a vision that sees beyond the stars and yet cherishes the sanctity of creation in its entirety.

As humanity gazes upward, the cosmos beckons not as a void to be filled with human ambition, but as a shared home, rich with mystery and promise. In this vastness, the Catholic faith finds a renewed call to stewardship, recognizing in the depths of space the infinite creativity of God and the perpetual invitation to participate in that ongoing creation. The journey into space, then, is a pilgrimage of discovery, stewardship, and reverence, illuminated by the light of faith and guided by the principles of justice and love.

Thus, the contemplation and exploration of space offer a unique opportunity to deepen our understanding of Divine Providence and to practice the principles of Catholic social teaching on a cosmic scale. It challenges us to envision a future where the heavens, no less than the Earth, are treated as a sacred trust—a common home for all humanity, entrusted to our care by the Creator, and destined for the common good.

Catholicism and the Multiplanetary Human Species

As humanity stands on the brink of becoming a multiplanetary species, it behooves us to delve deeper into the theological implications of this monumental shift. Embarking on a journey that transcends our singular planetary domain challenges us not only scientifically and technologically but also spiritually and morally. The Catholic faith, with its rich tradition of engaging with the mysteries of the universe and humanity's place within it, offers profound insights into this new epoch of human existence.

The endeavor to establish human presence beyond Earth brings to the fore questions about God's creation and the extension of His providence in the vast cosmos. It's crucial to recognize that Catholic teaching holds that all creation is under the sovereignty of God and that His will and purpose encompass all realms of existence, seen and unseen (Catechism of the Catholic Church, 1992). Thus, the expansion of humanity into space does not escape God's providential care but is, in fact, part of the unfolding of His divine plan.

The notion of humans inhabiting other planets can be seen as a manifestation of humanity exercising its God-given role as stewards of creation. This stewardship, however, demands of us a profound sense of responsibility - not merely in the maintenance and care of what is entrusted to us but also in the ethical considerations that accompany such a momentous expansion. We are called to engage with other worlds in a manner that reflects our reverence for creation and acknowledges our place within a divine order that spans the entirety of the cosmos.

As we contemplate the prospect of becoming a multiplanetary species, it's essential to reflect on the mystery of the Incarnation. The Catholic faith professes that in Jesus Christ, God has definitively entered human history and the material universe. This mystery deepens our understanding of the cosmos as a realm graced by God's intimate presence. It suggests that our efforts to extend human presence across the solar system and beyond are ways in which the saga of salvation history continues to unfold across the spatial and temporal expanses of creation.

Salvation history extended to other planets raises intriguing theological questions. If we encounter intelligent life forms, how does the message of salvation through Jesus Christ speak to them? The Catholic intellectual tradition compels us to approach such questions with humility, acknowledging the limits of our understanding while affirming the universality of God's salvific will (Lumen Gentium, 1964).

Moreover, the Catholic Church's social teachings offer a framework for considering the common good in the context of space exploration. The principle of the common good, which emphasizes the good that is shared and beneficial for all members of a community, can guide our endeavors in space, ensuring that the benefits and resources of space are shared equitably and used in ways that promote the dignity and flourishing of all human beings.

Another critical consideration is the environmental ethics of colonizing other worlds. Just as the Church advocates for the stewardship of Earth's environment, so too must we extend this care to the environments of other planets and moons. Our dominion over creation is not a license for exploitation but a vocation to cultivate and protect, ensuring that space exploration is conducted in a manner that is sustainable and respects the integrity of creation.

In light of our potential future among the stars, it's important to remember that the Church has always been a proponent of scientific inquiry and discovery. The compatibility of faith and reason means that our expanding scientific knowledge and capabilities are not threats to faith but opportunities to deepen our understanding of the Creator's work and to marvel at the breadth and complexity of His creation.

The journey towards becoming a multiplanetary species will undoubtedly challenge our understanding of ourselves, our world, and our faith. Yet, it is precisely in facing these challenges that we are offered the chance to grow in wisdom and in our relationship with the Creator. The Catholic vision, with its deep respect for both faith and reason, provides a solid foundation upon which to build as we embark on this new phase of human history.

Engaging with other worlds will require us not only to apply the best of our technological and scientific knowledge but also to bring the depth of our spiritual heritage to bear. In doing so, we affirm that our exploration of the cosmos is not merely an outward journey but also an inward one, inviting us to reflect on the mystery of the human person, made in the image of God, and called to communion with Him and with all creation.

As we stand on this threshold, let us move forward with a sense of purpose and hope. The calling to be stewards of creation, to seek understanding, to foster the common good, and to walk humbly with our God extends to the furthest reaches of the universe. In our quest to become a multiplanetary species, we have the opportunity to live out these aspects of our Catholic faith in new and profound ways.

In conclusion, the venture into becoming a multiplanetary species is not just a human endeavor but a spiritual journey that invites deep reflection on our place in the universe, the nature of God's creation, and the extension of His providential care. It's a journey that, while presenting new challenges, also opens up new avenues for witnessing to the universal saving plan of God, who is the Creator and final end of all that exists.

Theological Considerations of Living Beyond Earth

The endeavor to transcend the limits of our earthly confines and venture into the vast expanse of space presents not only a monumental scientific challenge but also a profound theological inquiry. If humanity succeeds in becoming a multiplanetary species, what implications does this hold for our understanding of God's providence, creation, and the role of human beings within this grand cosmic framework? As we contemplate life beyond Earth, we are invited to engage with these questions through the lens of Catholic teaching, harmonizing our scientific ambitions with a deep spiritual reflection on our place in the universe.

Firstly, it is critical to acknowledge that the cosmos, in all its immensity, is a manifestation of God's infinite might and wisdom. Space exploration and the aspiration to inhabit other planets should not be seen as a challenge to divine sovereignty but rather as an expression of the human vocation to explore and steward creation. This vocation, embedded within the Catholic understanding of human dignity and purpose, propels us to extend the horizon of our knowledge and dominion, always with the acknowledgment that we are ultimately not the master but stewards of the universe (Genesis 1:28).

The concept of Providence is central to Catholic theology and offers essential insights into our quest for a multiplanetary existence. Providence, the divine guidance whereby God leads His creation toward its ultimate perfection, does not negate human freedom or scientific endeavor. Instead, it envelops these efforts in the overarching narrative of God's love for His creation. As humanity stretches its reach to other worlds, it does so under the gaze of Providence, aligning its scientific progress with the greater good and ultimate purpose fashioned by the Creator.

Living beyond Earth compels us to rethink our understanding of community and the universal call to solidarity. Catholic social teaching, which emphasizes the common good, subsidiarity, and the inherent dignity of every person, extends beyond the confines of our planet. These principles should guide our interactions not only among ourselves but also potentially with other forms of life we might encounter. The acknowledgment of a Creator invites us to see the universe as a fraternity of beings, all created by God, and thus deserving of respect and dignity.

The sacramental economy, which pertains to the tangible means of grace instituted by Christ, presents a unique area for theological reflection. The administration of sacraments, central to Catholic life, presupposes a community gathered in a specific place. The challenge of ensuring the regular celebration of sacraments on distant planets will require innovative pastoral responses, always grounded in the conviction that Christ has bound himself to His Church until the end of time, irrespective of the physical boundaries of its congregation.

Eschatological questions also arise when considering the expansion of human life to other planets. Catholic eschatology teaches about the last things: death, judgment, heaven, and hell. The potential of human settlement on other worlds invites contemplation on how these teachings apply within a radically enlarged spatial context. It underscores the universality of Christ's redemptive act and the reach of God's salvific will, extending beyond Earth to the entirety of creation.

The sinfulness of humanity, manifested in our history through acts of violence, exploitation, and environmental degradation, prompts cautionary reflection on our multiplanetary aspirations. While reaching for the stars, humanity must undertake a deep moral introspection to ensure that the mistakes of the past are not replicated on new worlds. The Catholic commitment to justice and peace should shape our approach, emphasizing that in every sphere of human activity— including space colonization—compassion, respect, and care for creation must prevail.

Divine revelation, as communicated through Scripture, does not explicitly address the concept of life beyond Earth. Yet, it opens the way for a dynamic engagement with the unknown, encouraging a posture of humility, wonder, and openness to the mysteries of God's creation. The Catholic tradition, rich in its capacity to dialogue with new realms of human knowledge, invites us to explore these mysteries with both reason and faith, recognizing that all truth ultimately leads to God.

The saints, with their rich diversity of experiences and insights, offer spiritual guidance as we navigate the unknown territories of space. Their lives, marked by courage, innovation, and deep faith, provide inspiration for the challenges we face in extending human presence to other planets. In their company, we are reminded that the journey toward the heavens is ultimately a pursuit of holiness, guided by the hope of participating more fully in the infinite goodness of God.

The Church's magisterium, which has consistently engaged with the questions raised by scientific progress, must continue to offer direction as humanity embarks on this new phase of exploration. The teachings of the Church, grounded in the Gospel and enriched by centuries of reflection, provide a moral compass that can guide the ethical complexities of establishing human communities beyond Earth.

In conclusion, the possibility of extending human life to other planets presents a profound opportunity for theological reflection. It challenges us to deepen our understanding of God's providence, the integrity of creation, and our ethical responsibilities as stewards of the cosmos. As we look toward a future beyond our planet, we are called to a renewed faith in the Creator, who guides us through the vast expanse of space, inviting us to share in the unfolding of His divine plan.

Salvation History Extended to Other Planets As humanity stands at the precipice of becoming a multiplanetary species, it beckons us to explore how salvation history, as understood within the Catholic tradition, might extend beyond our earthly confines. This inquiry does not diminish the centrality of Christ's incarnation, death, and resurrection but invites a broader contemplation of God's salvific plan in the vast expanse of the cosmos.

The Catholic Church, with its rich intellectual tradition, has long engaged with questions of science and faith, recognizing that truth is a unity. When considering the salvation narrative in the context of other planets, it is paramount to affirm that God, as the creator of all, extends His providential care to the whole universe. The Scriptures affirm that "In the beginning, God created the heavens and the earth" (Genesis 1:1), laying the foundation for a theological understanding that encompasses all of creation.

As humanity ventures further into space, encountering other worlds that might harbor life, it challenges us to reinterpret the scope of God's salvific will. Does the plan of salvation, revealed in Jesus Christ on Earth, apply to beings on other planets? This question compels us to delve deeper into the mysteries of God's universal willingness to save and the unique nature of Christ's incarnation.

One must consider the incarnation of Christ as a definitive event within human history on Earth, pivotal for salvation. Yet, this does not preclude God's ability to engage with other intelligent life forms in a manner suited to their own histories and capacities for understanding. God's omnipotence ensures His actions are not limited to the paradigms we understand from our human perspective.

The concept of extraterrestrial beings having their own unique relationships with God introduces complex theological considerations. The Catholic Church teaches that God desires the salvation of all beings capable of receiving His grace. Thus, if intelligent life exists elsewhere, it falls within God's providential plan, potentially involving other, unknown modes of revelation and salvation history suited to those beings.

This broadening of perspective does not undermine the significance of Christ's salvific act but highlights the unfathomable richness of God's mercy and the manifold ways God could choose to reveal Himself throughout the universe. It echoes the thought that God's creation is boundlessly imaginative and generous, extending far beyond human comprehension.

Theologically, this invites a humble acknowledgment of the limitations of our earthly vantage point. Just as the discovery of the New World expanded the European understanding of the globe in the 15th and 16th centuries, so too might encounters with extraterrestrial life expand our understanding of salvation history. It demands an openness to the Holy Spirit's guidance in discerning new chapters of God's plan for the cosmos.

Philosophically, such considerations push the boundaries of traditional metaphysics and ethics. They necessitate a reevaluation of concepts such as personhood, moral responsibility, and the nature of societies beyond Earth. These are vast, uncharted territories for Catholic theology but are not insurmountable with God's wisdom.

From a scientific perspective, the search for extraterrestrial life raises profound questions about life's origins, diversity, and ultimate end. Catholic thought, which embraces both faith and reason, can offer a unique lens through which to interpret these discoveries. It can articulate a vision of cosmic history that is both scientifically informed and theologically rich, recognizing the inherent worth and dignity of all God's creatures.

Consideration of salvation history extended to other planets also invites reflection on the unity and diversity of God's creation. Just as biodiversity on Earth reflects the creativity of the Divine, so too might the varieties of life and intelligences in the universe speak of God's grandeur. This invites a celebration of the cosmic liturgy, where all creation gives glory to God, each in their unique way.

As we ponder the possibilities of life beyond Earth and the extension of salvation history to other planets, we are called to a renewed sense of wonder and responsibility. We are stewards of God's creation, not only on this planet but in the broader context of the cosmos. This stewardship entails a commitment to the pursuit of knowledge, tempered by humility and guided by ethical considerations that respect the integrity of creation.

Ultimately, humanity's exploration of space and potential encounters with extraterrestrial life are part of a larger narrative of God's ongoing revelation to us. It is a journey that requires both the light of faith and the insights of reason. As we move forward, our understanding of salvation history and God's plan for the cosmos will undoubtedly evolve, but the central tenet of God's love and desire for communion with all creation remains unchanging.

In conclusion, extending salvation history to other planets challenges us to think broadly about God's creative freedom and the ways in which God's saving grace might be operative throughout the universe. It is an invitation to marvel at the mystery of God's providence, which is always greater than our understanding, and to participate more fully in the cosmic scope of God's redemptive plan.

Chapter 11: Ecological Ethics in Space Exploration

In embarking upon the celestial quest of space exploration, humanity extends its stewardship beyond the confines of Earth, reaching into the vastness of the cosmos. This stewardship, as envisioned through the lens of Catholic social teachings, demands a profound respect for creation. It calls for an ecological ethic that balances exploration with the preservation of the natural order within the heavenly realms. The universe, in its majestic expanse, mirrors the infinite grandeur of its Creator. As stewards, humans hold a duty to maintain the ecological balance of this grand creation, even as they traverse the stars.

Space exploration offers humanity a unique vantage point from which to contemplate the Creator's handiwork. As people journey across the cosmos, the necessity for an ecological conscience becomes paramount. This conscience, grounded in the respect for all creation, guides explorers to interact with the celestial bodies in a manner that honors the intrinsic value of the universe. The delicate balance of cosmic ecosystems, much like that of Earth's, commands a mindful approach to exploration and habitation.

The ethical considerations of space exploration must encompass the potential impact on extraterrestrial environments. Just as Earth's biosphere is protected by rigorous environmental ethics, so too should the untouched vistas of space be approached with caution and reverence. The introduction of Earth-born microbes or the extraction of extraterrestrial resources poses significant moral dilemmas. These actions may irrevocably alter other worlds, contravening the call to protect the cosmic order and respect the creator's work.

Catholic social teaching, with its emphasis on the common good and the responsible use of resources, offers pertinent insights for ecological ethics in space. The principle of the common good extends beyond Earth, advocating for a universal commonality that includes all of creation. As humans venture into space, they must consider the well-being of the entire cosmos, ensuring that their actions promote not only human interests but also the health of celestial bodies and potential life forms they may host.

The virtue of prudence plays a critical role in guiding the actions of space explorers and policymakers. Decisions regarding space missions, colonization, and resource utilization must be made with foresight, reflecting on the long-term consequences of human activity in space. This prudential approach ensures that the wonders of the cosmos can be explored and appreciated by future generations.

Furthermore, the concept of integral ecology, as highlighted in recent ecclesial documents, illuminates the interconnectedness of all creation. This perspective encourages a holistic approach to space exploration, where the protection of celestial environments is seen as integral to the health of Earth's ecosystem. Space exploration, in this view, becomes an extension of humanity's ecological responsibility, transcending planetary boundaries.

As humanity embarks on the quest to become a multiplanetary species, ethical considerations regarding the use of space resources come to the forefront. The equitable distribution of these resources, in adherence to the preferential option for the poor, ensures that the benefits of space exploration are shared by all humanity. This principle guards against the monopolization of space by the affluent, fostering a cosmic common good.

The transition of human beings to a multiplanetary existence raises profound questions about the continuity of moral and ethical responsibilities. Just as Catholic social teachings guide the ethical use of Earth's resources, they also extend to the stewardship of the new worlds humans seek to inhabit. The mandate to cultivate and care for creation spans the entire universe, calling for responsible governance and the preservation of celestial bodies in their natural state.

The exploration of space, while offering new realms for human habitation and resource extraction, must not lead to the commodification of the cosmos. The intrinsic value of the universe, as a testament to the Creator's work, supersedes its utility. In this regard, space exploration calls for a paradigm shift, where the pursuit of knowledge and the expansion of human frontiers are balanced with the ethical imperatives of conservation and reverence for creation.

In conclusion, as humanity ventures further into the cosmos, the principles of ecological ethics must illuminate the path. The stewardship of creation, inherited from the Creator, demands a respectful and prudent approach to exploring and inhabiting the universe. Through an adherence to ecological ethics, grounded in Catholic social teachings, humanity can fulfill its role as caretakers of the cosmos, ensuring the preservation of the celestial order for future generations.

The ethical journey through space is not solely a quest for new worlds, but a pilgrimage inspired by a deep reverence for all creation. It is a testament to the belief that the universe, in all its wonder and mystery, is a sacred trust bestowed by the Creator, demanding of humanity the utmost care and respect. As stewards of this heavenly inheritance, the responsibility rests upon humanity to forge an ethical path that honors the Creator's work, ensuring that the cosmic order is maintained, and the beauty of creation is preserved for eternity.

Catholic Social Teachings and Sustainability in Space

As humanity reaches further into the cosmos, the integration of Catholic social teachings with sustainability in space emerges as a vital consideration for ethical exploration and habitation beyond Earth. The Church's teachings, rooted in respect for God's creation and a commitment to the common good, provide a framework that can guide these endeavors, ensuring that space exploration aligns with moral and ethical principles.

At the heart of Catholic social teaching is the principle of stewardship. This principle recognizes Earth and, by extension, the cosmos, as a collective gift from God. It is a gift that humanity is called to manage responsibly, protecting its integrity for current and future generations. As we venture into space, this stewardship role extends to other planets, moons, and celestial bodies, where the potential for life and the inherent value of pristine cosmic environments demand our respect and care.

The concept of the common good also holds significant implications for space exploration. This principle posits that the fruits of exploration and discovery should serve not just a privileged few but the entire human race. For instance, the advancements in technology, resources, and knowledge derived from space endeavors must be shared equitably, contributing to the betterment of people's lives irrespective of nationality, race, or economic status.

Solidarity is another cornerstone of Catholic social teaching, stressing the importance of connection and mutual support among all people. In the context of space, this solidarity urges collaboration among nations and peoples in exploring the heavens. The challenges of space exploration—ranging from technological to environmental—can't be tackled by any single entity or country. Instead, a cooperative approach, inspired by solidarity, promises the most ethical and effective way forward.

The preferential option for the poor, a preferential concern in Catholic teaching, introduces a unique perspective on space exploration's priorities. In planning missions and allocating the benefits of space resources, the needs of the most vulnerable and marginalized on Earth must be prioritized. This approach ensures that space exploration doesn't widen the gap between the rich and the poor but instead contributes to reducing it.

Subsidiarity and the role of government in space exploration cannot be overlooked. According to this principle, larger entities should not usurp the functions that can be effectively carried out by smaller entities. In applying this to space, it suggests that while governments have a critical role in facilitating and regulating space exploration, private entities and the wider community should also have opportunities to contribute and participate.

The principle of the dignity of the human person requires that all space exploration activities treat human participants with the utmost respect and care. This principle challenges us to consider the ethical treatment of astronauts, researchers, and possibly future settlers on other planets. Human dignity must remain at the forefront, dictating that the pursuit of knowledge never compounds human subjects to undue risk or exploitation.

As we consider the environmental ethics of space exploration, the principle of care for God's creation demands a cautious approach to the use, alteration, or potential contamination of extraterrestrial environments. Just as on Earth, we are called to protect the integrity of creation in space, preserving its beauty and wonder for future generations and, potentially, future forms of life.

Integral human development, a theme found throughout Catholic social teaching, emphasizes the need for a holistic approach to progress. In the space context, this means that technological and scientific advancements should be matched with ethical, cultural, and spiritual growth. The exploration of space should not only extend our physical reach but also deepen our understanding of creation's mystery and our responsibilities within it.

The challenge of sustainability in space demands an interdisciplinary and interfaith dialogue. Catholic social teaching offers valuable insights, but the conversation must also welcome scientific, philosophical, and ethical perspectives from across the spectrum of human thought.

With these principles as a guide, humanity can navigate the uncharted territories of space in a way that honors the Creator, respects creation, and promotes the common good. As we stand on the brink of becoming an interplanetary species, our actions in space must reflect our highest values and aspirations. The vast cosmos, a testament to God's providence and creativity, invites us not only to explore but to do so with humility, responsibility, and a deep sense of our place within the divine order.

In conclusion, Catholic social teachings provide a comprehensive ethical framework for sustainability in space exploration. By embracing stewardship, prioritizing the common good, living out solidarity, ensuring the dignity of all involved, and protecting the integrity of creation, we can venture beyond our planet in a manner that aligns with our deepest beliefs and values. The cosmos, a divine creation, calls us to explore with both awe and ethical earnestness, expanding our horizons while grounding our efforts in a profound respect for all of creation.

Maintaining Ecological Balance Across the Cosmos As the mantle of exploration extends beyond the cradle of Earth, the critical task of maintaining an ecological balance across the cosmos emerges as a paramount concern. This undertaking, deeply intertwined with our stewardship duties, calls for a synthesis of scientific prudence, philosophical wisdom, and biblical stewardship. In grappling with the immense responsibility of extending human activity to other planets and celestial bodies, the contemplation of creation through the lens of Catholic teaching provides a moral compass. Within this framework, Providence serves as the guiding principle, emphasizing that all creation is under God's sovereign care and direction.

The pursuit of understanding and engaging with the cosmos should be harmonized with the respect and awe due to God's creation. From the luminous stellar nurseries to the barren surfaces of distant moons, each part of the cosmos is a testament to the Creator's grandeur. As custodians of creation, the imperative to maintain ecological balance is not restricted to Earth's biosphere but extends to the entirety of the cosmos. This stewardship reflects an acknowledgment of the delicate interdependence of all created entities, a theme pervasive in Catholic social teachings.

Exploration and utilization of space resources must thus adhere to principles that prevent the degradation and exploitation of these cosmic environments. The physical universe, replete with wonders and potentialities, is also marked by fragility. Human activity, spurred by an insatiable curiosity and ambition, stands at a juncture where it can either uphold the cosmic order or inflict irreversible damage.

When considering human settlements on other worlds, the task of maintaining ecological balance assumes new dimensions. The introduction of Earth life to extraterrestrial environments, intentional or accidental, must be approached with caution. The ethical implications of such actions are profound, touching upon the intrinsic value of alien ecosystems, whether teeming with life or desolate.

The concept of the "common home," as articulated in Catholic social teaching, extends beyond Earth, enveloping the cosmos. This universal home, entrusted to humanity, demands a responsible approach to colonization and resource extraction. The potential for space to become a theater of exploitation and disregard for ecological balance must be counteracted with policies and practices that reflect an ethos of care and respect.

Providence, as understood within the Catholic tradition, provides a framework for viewing the cosmos as a continuum of

God's creative act. Human actions, in exploring and potentially altering extraterrestrial environments, operate within the purview of Divine Providence. This perspective does not absolve humans of responsibility but rather underscores the duty to act as instruments of God's will, fostering harmony and balance in all endeavors.

The colonization of other worlds, a subject once relegated to the domain of science fiction, now presents tangible ethical dilemmas. The interplay between advancing human civilization and preserving ecological integrity in extraterrestrial contexts prompts a reevaluation of what it means to be stewards of creation. The biblical injunction to "till and keep" the garden extends to the entire cosmos, challenging humanity to nurture and protect, not merely exploit.

In this cosmic journey, the Catholic Church has the opportunity to offer guidance informed by centuries of theological and moral reflection. Just as the Church has navigated the challenges and opportunities posed by scientific advancements throughout history, its role in the age of cosmic exploration is critical. The teachings on stewardship, the common good, and the sanctity of creation can illuminate the path forward.

Addressing the ecological ethics of space exploration requires a concerted effort that spans disciplines. Scientists, theologians, ethicists, and policymakers must collaborate to devise strategies that uphold the integrity of extraterrestrial ecosystems. This multidisciplinary approach is essential in crafting a coherent ethical framework that respects both the scientific imperatives and the moral dimensions of space exploration.

The dialogues between faith and reason, as exemplified in the interactions between Catholicism and the sciences, offer a fertile ground for addressing the complexities of maintaining ecological balance in space. These dialogues can pave the way for a holistic understanding of humanity's place in the cosmos and the responsibilities that accompany our exploratory endeavors.

In conclusion, the challenge of maintaining ecological balance across the cosmos invites humanity to a deeper contemplation of our relationship with creation. It calls for an integration of scientific excellence, ethical foresight, and spiritual wisdom, guided by the principle of Providence. As humanity stands on the brink of becoming a multiplanetary species, our actions must reflect a commitment to the flourishing of all creation, honoring the Creator and safeguarding the integrity of the cosmic "common home."

The endeavor to maintain ecological balance in the cosmos is both a scientific and spiritual journey. It is a testament to the human spirit's capacity for wonder, tempered by the humility of recognizing our place within the broader creation. As we venture further into the stars, may we carry forward the lessons of stewardship and respect, ensuring that the cosmos remains a vibrant testament to the grandeur of its Creator.

The Church and the Future of Space Travel

As humanity stands on the brink of becoming a multiplanetary species, the Roman Catholic Church finds itself at a pivotal juncture, mediating between ancient doctrines and the unfolding saga of human expansion into the cosmos. This endeavor, vast and ambitious, does not merely concern the logistical or scientific aspects; it beckons a profound reflection on spiritual, ethical, and theological grounds. The future of space travel, therefore, is not just a challenge to mankind's ingenuity but a call to introspect on our relationship with the Creator and His creation.

The Church's engagement with the cosmos is not new. In the grand narrative of Catholic tradition, the universe has always been seen as a testament to God's infinite power and wisdom. As humanity propels itself into the unknown, it is essential to remember that this venture into space does not detract from the sovereignty of the Divine but rather magnifies the grandeur of His creation.

From the earth to the furthest galaxy, all of creation sings a hymn to the glory of God. Space travel, in this context, is an extension of humanity's vocation to explore and steward the Creator's gift. Yet, as we venture beyond our terrestrial home, the ethical imperatives that have guided human action within the biosphere must also find their application in the vastness of space. The principles of justice, the common good, and the integrity of creation retain their relevance, irrespective of the celestial body we find ourselves on (Catholic Church, 1993).

The call to preserve the integrity of creation demands a sustainable approach to space exploration. The exploitation of extraterrestrial resources, the contamination of pristine worlds, and the disregard for potential extraterrestrial life forms are issues that require careful moral scrutiny. The Church's teaching on ecological ethics, as expounded in Laudato Si, offers a blueprint for responsible stewardship that transcends the bounds of Earth (Francis, 2015).

In contemplating the future of space travel, the notion of Divine Providence occupies a central place. The belief that God governs the universe with wisdom and love reassures that human endeavors in space fall within the ambit of His providential plan. This, however, should not lead to fatalism or passivity. Instead, it should inspire a cooperative attitude with Providence, aligning human aspirations in space with the ultimate good willed by God.

The Church's contribution to the ethics of space travel extends beyond cautionary principles; it also offers a vision of hope and unity. The endeavor to become a multiplanetary species, fraught with challenges and uncertainties, can become a conduit for global cooperation, transcending divisions of nationality, race, and creed. In this, the Church sees a reflection of the universal call to communion, a fundamental tenet of Catholic doctrine.

Furthermore, the Catholic intellectual tradition, with its rich heritage of engaging with science and philosophy, provides a robust framework for addressing the novel questions posed by space travel. The conceptual tools for navigating the ethical quandaries of interstellar exploration can be found within the Church's teachings on human dignity, the common good, and moral action.

As we look towards the future, the Church's role as a moral and spiritual beacon remains indispensable. It is through engagement and dialogue with the scientific community that a holistic understanding of space travel can be developed. This partnership, rooted in mutual respect and a shared commitment to the betterment of humanity, will be critical as we chart the path forward.

The sacramental imagination of the Catholic faith, which sees the presence of the divine in the material world, offers a unique perspective on the sanctity of the cosmos. This sacramentality invites a reverence for all of creation, instilling a sense of wonder and responsibility as humanity explores the heavens.

In the project of making humans a multiplanetary species, the Church sees an opportunity for existential reflection. The vastness of space and the potential discovery of life beyond Earth invite questions about the place of humanity in the universe and the scope of salvation history. These are questions that the Church, with its long history of theological and philosophical inquiry, is well-placed to address.

Space travel also poses practical challenges for the practice of faith. As humans establish communities beyond Earth, the Church must consider how to minister to the spiritual needs of the faithful in environments vastly different from our planetary cradle. This will require both creativity and fidelity to the Gospel, ensuring that the Church remains a source of light and guidance, even in the outer reaches of the solar system.

Lastly, the future of space travel will test the Church's commitment to social justice. The benefits and burdens of space exploration must be distributed equitably, ensuring that the new frontier does not become a preserve of the affluent but a shared heritage of all humanity. The Church's social teachings, with their emphasis on the preferential option for the poor and the universal destination of goods, will be essential in guiding these discussions.

In conclusion, the Church and the future of space travel are inextricably linked. As humanity reaches out to the stars, the Church's teachings offer a compass for navigating the moral and spiritual dimensions of this new era. Through a blend of faith and reason, hope and caution, the Church can help ensure that space travel opens new horizons for humanity without losing sight of our ultimate destination—the Kingdom of God.

Contributions of Catholic Thought to Interstellar Ethics

The exploration of space, with all its scientific and technological advancements, compels us to confront enduring ethical questions. The Catholic intellectual tradition, rooted in a deep understanding of natural law and divine revelation, offers critical insights into these inquiries. As humanity stands on the brink of becoming a multiplanetary species, it's imperative that we reflect on the guidance that the Catholic perspective can provide in navigating the unchartered moral territories of interstellar ethics.

At the heart of Catholic thought lies the principle that creation, in all its splendor, reflects the grandeur of its Creator. The universe, vast and beautiful, is not a mere accident of matter, but a testament to divine providence (Catechism of the Catholic Church, 1994). This mindset fosters a profound respect for the cosmos not merely as an expanse to be conquered, but as a creation to be revered. When considering the ethical implications of space exploration, this reverence must underpin our decisions, ensuring that our pursuits beyond Earth honor the sanctity of the cosmos as part of God's creation.

Stewardship, a concept deeply embedded in Catholic social teaching, further informs our ethical approach to interstellar endeavors. Just as we are called to care for Earth, our common home, this duty extends beyond our planetary boundaries to the entire universe. This stewardship compels us to explore space responsibly, mindful of the impact our actions may have on celestial bodies and possible extraterrestrial ecosystems (Pontifical Council for Justice and Peace, 2004). The pursuit of knowledge about the cosmos, while noble, must not come at the expense of the integrity of creation.

The principle of the common good, another cornerstone of Catholic ethics, has profound implications for space exploration. The benefits derived from venturing into space should serve not only those directly involved but the entirety of humanity, especially the most vulnerable among us. This principle challenges the notion of space as a frontier for the exploitation by the few, advocating instead for a collective approach that seeks to share the fruits of space exploration equitably (Pontifical Council for Justice and Peace, 2004).

The concept of solidarity, intrinsic to Catholic social teaching, extends to our treatment of potential alien life forms. Recognizing the inherent dignity of all creation, Catholic thought urges us to approach other beings with respect and compassion, fostering an ethic of peaceful coexistence and mutual respect. Should we encounter extraterrestrial life, this principle dictates a response marked not by domination, but by a desire for dialogue and understanding.

The Catholic tradition also offers guidance on the use of technology in space exploration. While recognizing the incredible potential of technology to extend our knowledge and capabilities, Catholic teaching urges us to temper our enthusiasm with prudence. The drive to advance technologically must not eclipse our ethical obligations or our commitment to safeguard creation. Technologies employed in space must be evaluated not only for their utility but also for their potential impact on the cosmic order and moral fabric.

As we venture further into the cosmos, the Catholic virtue of hope serves as a beacon. This hope, rooted in faith in God's providence, encourages us to face the unknown with confidence and trust, grounded in the belief that our explorations can contribute to the unfolding of God's plan for creation. This hope is not naive or unfounded but is supported by the conviction that our endeavors in space can further reveal the majesty of the Creator and deepen our appreciation for the wonder of creation.

Moreover, the sacramental vision of the universe, as viewed through the lens of Catholic sacramentality, suggests that the material reality of the cosmos can mediate God's grace. Through our interactions with the cosmos—studying its mysteries and ensuring its care—we participate in a dialogue with the divine, uncovering deeper spiritual truths and drawing closer to the Creator. The universe, in this perspective, becomes a sacramental space, where the sacred and the secular intersect, inviting us to encounter God through the very act of exploration.

In considering the colonization of other worlds, Catholic ethics insists on the importance of maintaining the dignity and rights of all involved parties, human and potentially non-human alike. The expansion of human presence into space must be guided by principles of justice, ensuring that new societies beyond Earth reflect the values of equality, dignity, and respect for life that are central to Catholic teaching.

Furthermore, the Catholic intellectual tradition, with its emphasis on the integration of faith and reason, offers a unique perspective on the role of science and faith in space exploration. Rather than viewing them as opposed realms, Catholic thought sees science and faith as complementary ways of understanding the universe. This integration ensures that our scientific pursuits in space are grounded in a moral and spiritual framework that respects both the Creator and creation.

The challenge of environmental stewardship, already significant on Earth, takes on new dimensions in the context of space. Catholic teaching on the environment underscores the critical need to protect and preserve the cosmic environment, safeguarding celestial bodies from pollution, exploitation, and damage. This commitment to ecological ethics in space reflects a broader understanding of our responsibility to care for creation in all its forms.

The concept of universality in Catholic thought also has profound implications for interstellar ethics. In recognizing the universal destination of goods, Catholic ethics prompts us to consider the resources of space as gifts to be shared equitably among all of humanity. This perspective challenges any claims of sovereignty over extraterrestrial territories or resources, advocating instead for a cooperative approach to the stewardship of the cosmos.

In navigating the ethical complexities of interstellar exploration, the virtue of prudence is indispensable. Catholic teaching on prudence as the ability to discern the proper course of action in uncertain situations becomes particularly relevant as we make decisions that could impact the future of humanity and the cosmos. This discernment, informed by a deep understanding of moral principles and the common good, guides us in forging a path that is both bold and ethical.

Finally, Catholic thought on the eschatological dimension of creation offers a perspective that transcends the immediate concerns of space exploration. Viewing the cosmos within the context of God's salvific plan reminds us that our ventures into space are part of a larger narrative of creation, fall, redemption, and glorification. This eschatological vision encourages us to approach space exploration with humility, recognizing that our efforts are ultimately directed towards the fulfillment of God's purposes for all creation.

In conclusion, Catholic thought provides a robust framework for addressing the ethical challenges of interstellar ethics. By grounding our exploration of space in principles of stewardship, respect for creation, the common good, and hope, we can navigate the vastness of the cosmos in a way that honors both our Creator and the creation entrusted to our care. As humanity embarks on this monumental journey, the Catholic intellectual tradition serves as a guiding light, illuminating the path toward a future where our celestial endeavors reflect the depth of our moral and spiritual convictions.

Guiding Principles for Future Missions As we venture further into the universe, the need for a compass that aligns with both our scientific ambitions and our spiritual values has never been more pressing. This alignment ensures that our cosmic explorations are not merely acts of human will and curiosity but are also reflective of a deeper understanding of our place in the creation and our duty to it. The following principles are proposed to guide future missions in a manner that honors both the quest for knowledge and our perennial Catholic teachings.

The first principle is that of *recognition of the cosmos as creation*. This implies acknowledging the universe in its vastness and complexity as a testament to God's grandeur. Approaching space exploration with this mindset fosters a profound respect for the cosmos not merely as a frontier to be conquered or exploited but as a divine creation to be honored and studied. This perspective encourages missions that are designed with a sense of stewardship and reverence, reframing our role in the universe as caretakers rather than proprietors.

Stewardship of the universe emerges as a second principle. This extends the Catholic duty of stewardship to include not only Earth but all celestial bodies and the space between them. Future missions must prioritize the protection and preservation of the cosmic environment, avoiding the contamination of planets and moons, and preventing the celestial equivalent of colonial exploitation.

The third principle involves the *pursuit of the common good*. Space exploration should be pursued not for the glory of one nation or a select few individuals but as a collective human endeavor that benefits all of humanity. This includes sharing the knowledge gained from space exploration openly and ensuring that the advancements and technologies developed are accessible to all countries, not just the technologically advanced ones.

Respect for possible extraterrestrial life forms the fourth principle. In our search for life beyond Earth, we must prepare to encounter it with the utmost respect for its intrinsic value and autonomy. This principle calls for protocols that ensure our explorations do not harm or disrupt potential alien ecosystems or societies.

Following closely is the principle of *humility in the face of the cosmos*. Recognizing the limits of human understanding and capability should be inherent in our spacefaring ethos. This principle advocates for missions that seek to learn and observe rather than dominate or control, acknowledging that the universe operates by God's laws, which we strive to understand but must ultimately respect.

A sixth guiding principle is the *integration of science and spirituality*. Future missions should embody a dialogue between the technological and spiritual dimensions of humanity. This involves seeing space exploration as a vocation that can bring us closer to understanding God's creation and our place within it, rather than as a purely secular endeavor.

The final principle rests on *hope and responsibility in our cosmic journey*. Space exploration must be driven by hope in the possibilities of what lies beyond our planet and a sense of responsibility for the legacy we leave. This includes not only the physical footprints left on other worlds but also the moral and ethical imprint of our actions as we step into the cosmos.

Implementing these principles requires a concerted effort from all stakeholders involved in space exploration, including governments, private companies, scientific communities, and religious organizations. It calls for policies that reflect these values, education that reinforces them, and missions that embody them.

As humanity stands on the cusp of becoming a multiplanetary species, these guiding principles provide a framework to ensure that our expansion into the cosmos is not only a triumph of technological achievement but also a testament to our growth as moral and spiritual beings. In doing so, future missions can truly reflect the glory of God's creation and our role within it as explorers who honor the Creator by respecting the majesty of the cosmos.

It is our hope and prayer that as we venture further into the stars, we carry with us the humility, reverence, and love that ground us in our faith. May our explorations always reflect our ultimate purpose—to glorify God and find Him in all things, for in Him, we move and have our being, even beyond the bounds of Earth.

In sum, the journey into the cosmos is not only a physical or technological endeavor but a deeply spiritual one that calls for a renewal of our commitment to God's creation and an expansion of our moral horizons. As we embark on this awe-inspiring journey, let us ensure that our guiding principles lead us closer to both the Creator and His creation.

Looking Heavenward with Hope and Responsibility

As we stand on the cusp of interstellar discovery, propelled by an insatiable curiosity that stretches back to the dawn of time, it is imperative that we reflect on the journey that humanity has embarked upon. Space exploration, a testament to human ingenuity and determination, gestures towards infinity with a mix of hope and responsibility. This pursuit, while exhilarating, brings to the fore a profound question rooted in the heart of both faith and science: How do we look heavenward, not just with the ambition to soar among the stars, but with a sense of our place in the cosmos as ordained by God?

In these times of remarkable endeavours beyond our planet, our contemplation of the heavens calls for a harmonious blend of awe at God's creation and a humble recognition of our role within it. The vast expanse above us, replete with galaxies, stars, and potential worlds beyond our own, does not solely represent an uncharted territory for our technologies to conquer. Instead, it signifies a divine creation, a universe teeming with wonders that speak silently of God's grandeur and providence. This dual acknowledgement forms the cornerstone of our hope and responsibility as we gaze heavenward.

While the pursuit of knowledge is an innate human trait, our explorations must be grounded in ethical considerations that respect the inherent sanctity of the cosmos as part of God's creation. As stewards of the universe, our ventures into space carry with them the weight of responsibility to maintain ecological balance and respect for all creation, a principle deeply embedded in Catholic social teachings.

This stewardship extends beyond mere conservation, enveloping a moral imperative to safeguard the dignity of every aspect of the cosmos. Engaging with the expansive vistas of space, humans are challenged to transcend their transient desires, approaching this new frontier not as conquerors but as humble seekers of wisdom and understanding.

The Church's dialogue with science serves as a bridge between faith and reason, celebrating the wonders of the cosmos as signposts to the Divine. This dialogue encourages a posture of humility and wonder, acknowledging our limited understanding while embracing the mystery of creation. It is through this lens of faith and reason that we must navigate the ethical complexities of cosmic exploration, ensuring that our actions honor the Creator and the intrinsic value of his creation.

In embracing our cosmic journey, we are called to expand our horizons, not only spatially but spiritually. The vastness of space and the potential of discovering new worlds invite us to ponder our place in the universe and the continuous unfolding of salvation history. This expansion of our physical and spiritual frontiers enables us to encounter God in new and profound ways, reaffirming our faith and our commitment to His creation.

As we venture forth, the concept of space as a common home emerges as a crucial ethical guideline. This notion, reminiscent of the imperative to care for our Earth, underscores the importance of shared stewardship and the avoidance of exploiting celestial bodies for the benefit of a few. The heavens, in their majestic expanse, are a gift to all humanity, requiring a collective and responsible approach to exploration and habitation.

The potential colonization of other worlds prompts us to consider the theological implications of a multiplanetary human species. These considerations call for a deep reflection on our understanding of salvation history and the universality of Christ's redemption. The Gospel message, while rooted in the history of our world, speaks to the entire cosmos, offering a beacon of hope and a call to universal brotherhood as we step into the unknown.

Our responsibility towards creation, as emphasized by Catholic ecological ethics, extends beyond our atmospheric confines, demanding a commitment to sustainability and balance across the cosmos. The lessons learned from caring for our planet provide invaluable insights into how we might approach the stewardship of other worlds, ensuring that our cosmic journey is marked by respect and responsibility.

The contributions of Catholic thought to interstellar ethics offer guiding principles for future missions, highlighting the importance of a moral compass in navigating the challenges of space travel. These principles, founded on the dignity of creation and the common good, serve as a foundation for ethical exploration and colonization.

As we look heavenward, our aspirations for discovery and understanding are tempered by an unwavering commitment to uphold the sanctity of the cosmos as a creation of God. The awe-inspiring vastness of space calls us to a greater awareness of our smallness and yet, paradoxically, to an appreciation of our unique role as co-creators with God, tasked with the stewardship of His magnificent creation.

In conclusion, the journey to the stars, fueled by both hope and responsibility, beckons us to tread with humility, wisdom, and a profound reverence for creation. It invites us to look beyond the transient and to see in the fabric of the cosmos the hand of God, guiding us towards an understanding that integrates faith, science, and an ethical commitment to the universe. This journey, a synthesis of human aspiration and divine providence, points us towards a future where heaven and earth converge in the shared pursuit of knowledge, grounded in the love and respect of God's creation.

May our exploration of the heavens be ever guided by a sense of wonder, responsibility, and ethical stewardship, ensuring that as we reach for the stars, we remain firmly rooted in the teachings of the Church and the enduring love of the Creator. As we look heavenward, let us do so with hope, guided by the light of faith and the knowledge that in every corner of the cosmos, we are in the presence of the Almighty.

References:

Appendix A: Catholic Documents on Science and the Universe

The relationship between the Catholic Church and the scientific understanding of the universe has been marked by a journey of growth, reflection, and dialogue. The teachings of the Church, rooted in the belief that God is the almighty Creator and the final end of all creation, provide a framework that embraces the inquiry into the cosmos and the pursuit of truth that characterizes scientific endeavor. This appendix explores key Catholic documents that illuminate the Church's stance on science and the cosmos, serving as a guide for believers and scholars navigating the confluence of faith and cosmic exploration.

In recent years, the Magisterium has sought to address the profound questions arising from advancements in astronomy and the possibility of humans becoming a multiplanetary species. At the heart of these discussions has been a reaffirmation of the divine providence that governs the universe, a principle deeply embedded in Catholic thought. The documents presented here span a range of topics, from the ethical implications of space exploration to the stewardship of the cosmos as part of God's creation.

One seminal text in understanding the Church's view on the universe and science is *Fides et Ratio* (Faith and Reason) by Saint Pope John Paul II (1998). In this encyclical, the Pope elucidates the complementary relationship between faith and reason, asserting that the pursuit of truth in scientific inquiry is not only compatible with faith but is also a reflection of the human desire to understand the Creator through His creation. The Pope argues that the natural world, including the vast expanse of space, is an open book in which the signs of God's grandeur are imprinted.

Another pivotal document is the address of Pope Francis to the Pontifical Academy of Sciences (2014), where he speaks directly to the responsibilities that come with technological and scientific advancement. Pope Francis emphasizes the necessity of ethical considerations in the exploration of the universe, calling for a stewardship that respects creation and promotes the common good. This address echoes the sentiments expressed in Laudato Si' (2015), an encyclical that, while focused on Earth's environment, also touches upon humanity's relationship with the cosmos at large, urging a harmonious existence that mirrors the Creator's care and concern for all of creation.

The Vatican Observatory has also been a significant voice in the dialogue between the Catholic Church and the scientific community. As one of the oldest astronomical research institutions in the world, its work exemplifies the Church's dedication to understanding the universe. The Observatory's scholars, many of whom are priests and brothers, contribute to the field of astronomy while embodying the belief that scientific inquiry is a path to greater appreciation of God's creative work.

The exploration of space presents unique challenges and opportunities for applying Catholic social teaching. The potential for colonizing other worlds, as discussed in various Vatican communications, brings to the forefront issues of justice, equity, and the sanctity of life in all forms. These writings suggest that the same principles guiding human behavior on Earth should also shape our actions as we reach beyond our planet.

In the quest for knowledge and the expansion of human presence in the universe, the Church champions a responsible and ethical approach. Documents emphasize the need to balance scientific progress with respect for creation, underscoring the belief that the cosmos, in all its mystery and beauty, is a testament to the infinite wisdom and love of its Creator.

Through these documents, the Church calls on scientists, cosmologists, and believers alike to consider not just the how of cosmic exploration, but also the why. They encourage a reflective journey that not only seeks to unravel the mysteries of the universe but also to understand our place within it, guided by reverence for life and a commitment to the well-being of all creation.

At its core, the discussion about science and the universe in Catholic teaching is imbued with awe for the Creator's grand design. It fosters a dialogue that bridges faith and reason, challenging humanity to explore the cosmos with humility, hope, and responsibility. As stewards of creation, we are invited to look heavenward, not as conquerors but as caretakers, ensuring that our cosmic journey reflects the providential care that sustains the universe.

In conclusion, the Catholic Church recognizes and applauds the efforts to understand and explore the universe, seeing in these endeavors a reflection of the human spirit's innate desire to reach out to the Creator. By providing guidance through its teachings and encouraging ethical reflection, the Church plays a pivotal role in shaping the future of humanity's journey among the stars. These documents serve as a testament to the Church's ongoing commitment to dialogue with the scientific community, rooted in the belief that through the exploration of the cosmos, we draw nearer to comprehending the fullness of God's creation.

Glossary of Terms in Cosmology and Catholic Theology

In bridging the seemingly vast expanse between cosmology and Catholic theology, several pivotal terms emerge, weaving together the fabric of our understanding of the universe through the lenses of faith and science. This glossary seeks to illuminate these terms, offering a beacon for those navigating the confluence of celestial inquiry and spiritual contemplation.

Big Bang Theory

A cosmological model that explains the early development of the Universe, which posits that it expanded from a very high-density and high-temperature state. For Catholics, this theory is often viewed in harmony with divine creation, as it points to a moment of beginning congruent with the concept of a Creator.

Cosmology

The scientific study of the large-scale properties of the universe as a whole. It endeavors to understand the universe's origin, evolution, structure, and eventual fate. This discipline, while rooted in physics and astronomy, also intersects profoundly with theological questions about creation and existence.

Creation ex nihilo

A theological concept meaning "creation out of nothing." It denotes the belief that God created the world freely out of nothing, without the use of pre-existing materials. This doctrine underscores God's omnipotence and the dependence of all existence upon the Divine Will.

Divine Providence

The governance of God over the universe, directing creation towards its ultimate purpose and good. Providence is seen not as a denial of freedom but as a guiding hand ensuring that the cosmos and its laws lead to the fulfillment of God's plan.

Eschatology

In theology, eschatology refers to the study of "last things," including the end times, the Second Coming of Christ, the resurrection of the dead, and the Last Judgment. Cosmology echoes these themes in its exploration of the ultimate fate of the universe.

Exoplanet

A planet that orbits a star outside our solar system. The study of exoplanets holds profound implications for cosmology and theology, raising questions about the uniqueness of Earth and the potential for life elsewhere in the universe.

Light-year

A unit of astronomical distance equivalent to the distance that light travels in one year, which is about 9.461 trillion kilometers or 5.878 trillion miles. It serves as a reminder of the vastness of creation and the marvel of the universe's expanse.

Multiverse Theory

A theoretical framework suggesting the existence of multiple, perhaps infinite, universes including our own. This concept challenges and expands theological discussions concerning creation, divine action, and the uniqueness of our universe.

Natural Law

In Catholic theology, natural law refers to the reason's participation in God's eternal law. It's the objective order established by God that determines the requirements for humans to thrive and reach fulfillment. Cosmology aligns with this through the discovery of physical laws governing the universe.

Ontology

The branch of metaphysics dealing with the nature of being. In both theology and cosmology, ontology questions the essence of existence, the nature of the universe, and the concept of God.

Panspermia

A hypothesis proposing that life exists throughout the Universe, distributed by space dust, meteoroids, asteroids, comets, planetoids, or potentially by spacecraft in the form of unintentional contamination by microbes. This notion intersects intriguingly with theological considerations of life and creation.

Quantum Mechanics

A fundamental theory in physics that provides a description of the physical properties of nature at the scale of atoms and subatomic particles. Quantum mechanics introduces concepts that challenge traditional notions of causality and determinism and opens up new areas for dialogue between science and faith.

Red Shift

In cosmology, redshift is a phenomenon where light from an object moves towards the red end of the spectrum as it travels away from us. This concept is crucial for understanding the universe's expansion and supports the Big Bang Theory, contributing to discussions on the universe's temporal beginning.

Theological Anthropology

A field of theology that studies the nature of humanity from a Christian perspective. It examines questions of human origin, purpose, and destiny in the light of faith, often intersecting with cosmological insights into humanity's place in the universe.

Transcendence

In theology, transcendence refers to the aspect of God's nature and power which is wholly independent of the material universe, beyond all physical laws. This concept is vital for understanding the relationship between Creator and creation, highlighting the divine mystery that pervades cosmological exploration.

References

1. Genesis 1-2. The Holy Bible.

2. Hawking, S. (1988). A brief history of time: From the big bang to black holes. Bantam Books.

3. Vatican Observatory. (n.d.). Faith and Science.

4. Harrison, P. (2015). *The Territories of Science and Religion*. University of Chicago Press. This source explores the historical and conceptual relations between science and religion, offering insights into how the two can converge in the modern world.

5. Holder, R. D. (2013). *Big Bang, Big God: A Universe Designed for Life?* Lion Books.

6. Spitzer, R. J. (2010). *New Proofs for the Existence of God: Contributions of Contemporary Physics and Philosophy.* Eerdmans.

7. Genesis 1: 26-28

8. Catechism of the Catholic Church. (1994). Vatican City: Libreria Editrice Vaticana.

9. Catechism of the Catholic Church. (1997). 2nd ed. Libreria Editrice Vaticana.

10. Pontifical Biblical Commission. (1993). The Interpretation of the Bible in the Church. Libreria Editrice Vaticana.

11. Consolmagno, G. J., & Mueller, P. R. (2014). *Would You Baptize an Extraterrestrial?: . . . and Other Questions from the Astronomers' In-box at the Vatican Observatory*. Image.

12. United States Conference of Catholic Bishops. (2003). *For I Was Hungry and You Gave Me Food: Catholic Reflections on Food, Farmers, and Farmworkers*. USCCB.

13. Catechism of the Catholic Church. (1992). Vatican: Libreria Editrice Vaticana.

14. Pope Francis. (2015). Laudato Si': On care for our common home. Vatican: Libreria Editrice Vaticana.

15. Pontifical Academy of Sciences. (2009). The Scientific Legacy of the 20th Century. Vatican City.

16. United States Conference of Catholic Bishops. (n.d.). *Catholic Social Teaching on Care for Creation and Stewardship of the Earth*. Retrieved from http://www.usccb.org/issues-and-action/human-life-and-dignity/environment/index.cfm

17. Genesis 1:28 (New Revised Standard Version).

18. *National Aeronautics and Space Administration. (2020). NASA's Artemis Program. Retrieved from https://www.nasa.gov/specials/artemis/*

19. *Scheid, D. P. (2016). The Cosmic Common Good: Religious Grounds for Ecological Ethics. United States: Oxford University Press.*

20. *John Paul II. (1991). Centesimus Annus. Vatican City: Libreria Editrice Vaticana.*

21. *Pontifical Council for Justice and Peace. (2004). Compendium of the Social Doctrine of the Church. Vatican City: Libreria Editrice Vaticana.*

22. *United Nations Office for Outer Space Affairs. (1967). Treaty on Principles Governing the Activities of States in the Exploration and Use of Outer Space, including the Moon and Other Celestial Bodies. Vienna: United Nations.*

23. McGrath, A. E. (2019). A Scientific Theology: Nature, Volume 1. Grand Rapids, MI: Eerdmans.

24. Ruse, M. (2018). Can a Darwinian be a Christian?: The Relationship between Science and Religion. Cambridge: Cambridge University Press.

25. Lumen Gentium. (1964). Dogmatic Constitution on the Church, Second Vatican Council.

26. Second Vatican Council. (1965). Gaudium et spes. Vatican City: Vatican Press.

27. *Genesis* 1:1. The Holy Bible.

28. John Paul II. (1988). *Address to the Pontifical Academy of Sciences.* Vatican.

29. Pius XII. (1950). *Humani Generis.* Vatican.

30. *National Aeronautics and Space Administration. (2020). NASA's Artemis Plan. NASA.*

31. *United Nations Office for Outer Space Affairs. (1967). Treaty on Principles Governing the Activities of States in the Exploration and Use of Outer Space, including the Moon and Other Celestial Bodies. United Nations.*

32. *The Church and the Challenges of Space Exploration: Proceedings of the Study Week on the Ethical and Religious Implications of Space Exploration.* The Vatican Observatory, 2020.

33. *Ecological Ethics and the Human Soul: Aquinas, Whitehead, and the Metaphysics of Value.* University of Notre Dame Press, 2021.

34. Pontifical Council for Justice and Peace. (2004). Compendium of the Social Doctrine of the Church. Vatican City: Libreria Editrice Vaticana.

35. Pope John Paul II. (1998). *Fides et Ratio.* Vatican City: Libreria Editrice Vaticana.

36. Pope Francis. (2014). Address to the Pontifical Academy
of Sciences. Vatican City.

THE 15 PRAYERS OF ST. BRIDGET

 These Prayers and these Promises have been copied from a
book printed in Toulouse in 1740 and published by the P.
Adrien Parvilliers of the Company of Jesus, Apostolic
Missionary of the Holy Land, with approbation, permission
and recommendation to distribute them.
Pope Pius IX took cognisance of these Prayers with the
prologue; he approved them May 31, 1862, recognising
them as true and for the good of souls.

As St. Bridget for a long time wanted to know the number of
blows Our Lord received during His Passion, He one day
appeared to her and said: "I received 5480 blows on My
Body. If you wish to honour them in some way, say 15 Our
Fathers and 15 Hail Marys with the following Prayers (which
He taught her) for a whole year. When the year is up, you
will have honoured each one of My Wounds."

He made the following promises to anyone who recited these Prayers for a whole year:

1. I will deliver 15 souls of his lineage from Purgatory.

2. 15 souls of his lineage will be confirmed and preserved in grace.

3. 15 sinners of his lineage will be converted.

4. Whoever recites these Prayers will attain the first degree of perfection.

5. 15 days before his death I will give him My Precious Body in order that he may escape eternal starvation; I will give him My Precious Blood to drink lest he thirst eternally.

6. 15 days before his death he will feel a deep contrition for all his sins and will have a perfect knowledge of them.

7. I will place before him the sign of My Victorious Cross for his help and defence against the attacks of his enemies.

8. Before his death I shall come with My Dearest Beloved Mother.

9. I shall graciously receive his soul, and will lead it into eternal joys.

10. And having led it there I shall give him a special draught from the fountain of My Deity, something I will not for those who have not recited My Prayers.

11. Let it be known that whoever may have been living in a state of mortal sin for 30 years, but who will

recite devoutly, or have the intention to recite these
Prayers, the Lord will forgive him all his sins.

12. I shall protect him from strong temptations.

13. I shall preserve and guard his 5 senses.

14. I shall preserve him from a sudden death.

15. His soul will be delivered from eternal death.

16. He will obtain all he asks for from God and the
    Blessed Virgin.

17. If he has lived all his life doing his own will and he is
    to die the next day, his life will be prolonged.

18. Every time one recites these Prayers he gains 100
    days indulgence.

19. He is assured of being joined to the supreme Choir
    of Angels.

20. Whoever teaches these Prayers to another, will have
    continuous joy and merit which will endure eternally.

21. There where these Prayers are being said or will be
    said in the future God is present with His grace.

**Each prayer is preceded by one Our Father and one
Hail Mary.**

Our Father, who art in heaven, hallowed be thy name.
Thy kingdom come.
Thy will be done on earth as it is in heaven.
Give us this day our daily bread and forgive us our
trespasses as we forgive those who trespass against us and

lead us not into temptation but deliver us from evil. **Amen**

Hail Mary, full of grace, the Lord is with thee; blessed art thou among women and blessed is the fruit of thy womb, Jesus.
Holy Mary, Mother of God, pray for us sinners, now and at the hour of our death. **Amen.**

FIRST PRAYER
Our Father – Hail Mary.
O Jesus Christ! Eternal Sweetness to those who love Thee, joy surpassing all joy and all desire, Salvation and Hope of all sinners, Who hast proved that Thou hast no greater desire than to be among men, even assuming human nature at the fullness of time for the love of men, recall all the sufferings Thou hast endured from the instant of Thy conception, and especially during Thy Passion, as it was decreed and ordained from all eternity in the Divine plan.

Remember, O Lord, that during the Last Supper with Thy disciples, having washed their feet, Thou gavest them Thy Most Precious Body and Blood, and while at the same time thou didst sweetly console them, Thou didst foretell them Thy coming Passion.
Remember the sadness and bitterness which Thou didst experience in Thy Soul as Thou Thyself bore witness saying: "My Soul is sorrowful even unto death."

Remember all the fear, anguish and pain that Thou didst suffer in Thy delicate Body before the torment of the Crucifixion, when, after having prayed three times, bathed in a sweat of blood, Thou wast betrayed by Judas, Thy disciple, arrested by the people of a nation Thou hadst chosen and elevated, accused by false witnesses, unjustly judged by three judges during the flower of Thy youth and during the solemn Paschal season.

Remember that Thou wast despoiled of Thy garments and

clothed in those of derision; that Thy Face and Eyes were
veiled, that Thou wast buffeted, crowned with thorns, a reed
placed in Thy Hands, that Thou was crushed with blows and
overwhelmed with affronts and outrages.
In memory of all these pains and sufferings which Thou didst
endure before Thy Passion on the Cross, grant me before my
death true contrition, a sincere and entire confession,
worthy satisfaction and the remission of all my sins. **Amen.**

SECOND PRAYER
Our Father – Hail Mary.
O Jesus! True liberty of angels, Paradise of delights,
remember the horror and sadness which Thou didst endure
when Thy enemies, like furious lions, surrounded Thee, and
by thousands of insults, spits, blows, lacerations and other
unheard-of-cruelties, tormented Thee at will.

In consideration of these torments and insulting words, I
beseech Thee, O my Saviour, to deliver me from all my
enemies, visible and invisible, and to bring me, under Thy
protection, to the perfection of eternal salvation. **Amen.**

THIRD PRAYER
Our Father – Hail Mary.
O Jesus! Creator of Heaven and earth Whom nothing can
encompass or limit, Thou Who dost enfold and hold all under
Thy Loving power, remember the very bitter pain.

Thou didst suffer when the Jews nailed Thy Sacred Hands
and Feet to the Cross by blow after blow with big blunt nails,
and not finding Thee in a pitiable enough state to satisfy
their rage, they enlarged Thy Wounds, and added pain to
pain, and with indescribable cruelty stretched Thy Body
on the Cross, pulled Thee from all sides, thus dislocating Thy
Limbs.

I beg of Thee, O Jesus, by the memory of this most Loving suffering of the Cross, to grant me the grace to fear Thee and to Love Thee. **Amen.**

FOURTH PRAYER
Our Father – Hail Mary.
O Jesus! Heavenly Physician, raised aloft on the Cross to heal our wounds with Thine, remember the bruises which Thou didst suffer and the weakness of all Thy Members which were distended to such a degree that never was there pain like unto Thine.

From the crown of Thy Head to the Soles of Thy Feet there was not one spot on Thy Body that was not in torment, and yet, forgetting all Thy sufferings, Thou didst not cease to pray to Thy Heavenly Father for Thy enemies, saying: "Father forgive them for they know not what they do."

Through this great Mercy, and in memory of this suffering, grant that the remembrance of Thy Most Bitter Passion may effect in us a perfect contrition and the remission of all our sins. **Amen**.

FIFTH PRAYER
Our Father – Hail Mary.
O Jesus! Mirror of eternal splendour, remember the sadness which Thou experienced, when contemplating in the light of Thy Divinity the predestination of those who would be saved by the merits of Thy Sacred Passion.

Thou didst see at the same time, the great multitude of reprobates who would be damned for their sins, and Thou didst complain bitterly of those hopeless lost and unfortunate sinners.

Through this abyss of compassion and pity, and especially

through the goodness which Thou displayed to the good thief when Thou saidst to him: "This day, thou shalt be with Me in Paradise." I beg of Thee, O Sweet Jesus, that at the hour of my death, Thou wilt show me mercy. **Amen**.

SIXTH PRAYER
Our Father – Hail Mary.
O Jesus! Beloved and most desirable King, remember the grief Thou didst suffer, when naked and like a common criminal.

Thou was fastened and raised on the Cross, when all Thy relatives and friends abandoned Thee, except Thy Beloved Mother, who remained close to Thee during Thy agony and whom Thou didst entrust to Thy faithful disciple when Thou saidst to Mary: "Woman, behold thy son!" and to St. John: "Son, behold thy Mother!"

I beg of Thee O my Saviour, by the sword of sorrow which pierced the soul of Thy holy Mother, to have compassion on me in all my affliction and tribulations, both corporal and spiritual, and to assist me in all my trials, and especially at the hour of my death. **Amen**.

SEVENTH PRAYER
Our Father – Hail Mary.
O Jesus! Inexhaustible Fountain of compassion, Who by a profound gesture of Love, said from the Cross: "I thirst!" suffered from the thirst for the salvation of the human race.

I beg of Thee O my Saviour, to inflame in our hearts the desire to tend toward perfection in all our acts; and to extinguish in us the concupiscence of the flesh and the ardor of worldly desires. **Amen**.

EIGHTH PRAYER
Our Father – Hail Mary.
O Jesus! Sweetness of hearts, delight of the spirit, by the bitterness of the vinegar and gall which Thou didst taste on the Cross for Love of us, grant us the grace to receive worthily.

Thy Precious Body and Blood during our life and at the hour of our death, that they may serve as a remedy and consolation for our souls. **Amen.**

NINTH PRAYER
Our Father – Hail Mary.
O Jesus! Royal virtue, joy of the mind, recall the pain Thou didst endure when, plunged in an ocean of bitterness at the approach of death, insulted, outraged by the Jews.

Thou didst cry out in a loud voice that Thou was abandoned by Thy Father, saying: "My God, My God, why hast Thou forsaken me?"

Through this anguish, I beg of Thee, O my Saviour, not to abandon me in the terrors and pains of my death. **Amen.**

TENTH PRAYER
Our Father – Hail Mary.
O Jesus! Who art the beginning and end of all things, life and virtue, remembers that for our sakes Thou was plunged in an abyss of suffering from the soles of Thy Feet to the crown of Thy Head.

In consideration of the enormity of Thy Wounds, teach me to keep, through pure love, Thy Commandments, whose way is wide and easy for those who love Thee. **Amen.**

ELEVENTH PRAYER
Our Father – Hail Mary.

O Jesus! Deep abyss of mercy, I beg of Thee, in memory of Thy Wounds which penetrated to the very marrow of Thy Bones and to the depth of Thy being, to draw me, a miserable sinner, overwhelmed by my offenses, away from sin and to hide me from Thy Face justly irritated against me, hide me in Thy wounds, until Thy anger and just indignation shall have passed away. **Amen.**

TWELFTH PRAYER
Our Father – Hail Mary.

O Jesus! Mirror of Truth, symbol of unity, bond of charity, remember the multitude of wounds with which Thou wast afflicted from head to foot, torn and reddened by the spilling of Thy adorable Blood. O great and universal pain, which Thou didst suffer in Thy virginal flesh for love of us! Sweetest Jesus! What is there that Thou couldst have done for us which Thou has not done!

May the fruit of Thy suffering be renewed in my soul by the faithful remembrance of Thy Passion, and may Thy love increase in my heart each day, until I see Thee in eternity: Thou Who art the treasure of every real good and every joy, which I beg Thee to grant me, O Sweetest Jesus, in heaven. **Amen.**

THIRTEENTH PRAYER
Our Father – Hail Mary.

O Jesus! Strong Lion, Immortal and Invincible King, remember the pain which Thou didst endure when all Thy strength, both moral and physical, was entirely exhausted, Thou didst bow Thy Head, saying: "It is consummated!"

Through this anguish and grief, I beg of Thee Lord Jesus, to have mercy on me at the hour of my death when my mind

will be greatly troubled and my soul will be in
anguish. **Amen.**

FOURTEENTH PRAYER
Our Father - Hail Mary.
O Jesus! Only Son of the Father, Splendour and Figure of His
Substance, remember the simple and humble
recommendation.

Thou didst make of Thy Soul to Thy Eternal Father, saying:
"Father, into Thy Hands I commend My Spirit!" And with Thy
Body all torn, and Thy Heart Broken, and the bowels of
Thy Mercy open to redeem us, Thou didst Expire.

By this Precious Death, I beg of Thee O King of Saints,
comfort me and help me to resist the devil, the flesh and the
world, so that being dead to the world I may live for Thee
alone.

I beg of Thee at the hour of my death to receive me, a
pilgrim and an exile returning to Thee. **Amen.**

FIFTEENTH PRAYER
Our Father - Hail Mary.
O Jesus! True and fruitful Vine! Remember the abundant
outpouring of Blood which Thou didst so generously shed
from Thy Sacred Body as juice from grapes in a wine press.

From Thy Side, pierced with a lance by a soldier, blood and
water issued forth until there was not left in Thy Body a
single drop, and finally, like a bundle of myrrh lifted to the
top of the Cross Thy delicate Flesh was destroyed, the very
Substance of Thy Body withered, and the Marrow of Thy
Bones dried up.

Through this bitter Passion and through the outpouring of

Thy Precious Blood, I beg of Thee, O Sweet Jesus, to receive my soul when I am in my death agony. **Amen.**

CONCLUSION
O Sweet Jesus! Pierce my heart so that my tears of penitence and love will be my bread day and night; may I be converted entirely to Thee, may my heart be Thy perpetual habitation, may my conversation be pleasing to Thee, and may the end of my life be so praiseworthy that I may merit Heaven and there with Thy saints, praise Thee forever. **Amen.**